P9-AGA-064

SEEING

CENTRAL
PARK

SEEING
CENTRAL
PARK

*The Official Guide to
the World's Greatest
Urban Park*

SARA CEDAR MILLER

*Abrams, New York
in association with the Central Park Conservancy*

CONTENTS

FOREWORD

The historic partnership of Frederick Law Olmsted and Calvert Vaux resulted in the creation of one of the most enduring and important works of art in America—Central Park. Now, more than a century and a half later, the Park is again graced with another historic partnership, that of the Central Park Conservancy—the non-profit organization that manages, restores, and maintains the Park—and the City of New York. Largely through the efforts of the Conservancy, Central Park has undergone a recent renaissance that may very well be New York City's greatest Cinderella story.

With private funding, improved technology, and innovative management practices, Central Park has never been more beautiful or better managed than it is today. The Conservancy is proud to be the leader of Central Park's longest period of sustained health and beauty. Not only do the following photographs highlight the brilliance of the Park's many designs, but also they are testimony to and evidence of the generous donors to the Conservancy, its dedicated trustees, volunteers, and staff—Sara Cedar Miller among them—who protect the Park today and will endeavor

Cascade in the Ravine

to meet its needs to survive and flourish for generations to come.

In her previous book—*Central Park, An American Masterpiece*, published by Abrams in 2003—Sara narrated the Park's fascinating history along with photographs of its magnificent landscapes, architecture, and sculptures, which had been restored and revitalized by the Conservancy's efforts up to that year.

In this book, we invite you to take an armchair tour (or travel on foot) with Sara as she guides you, through her words and images, to revisit those well-known wonderful Central Park features, learn about some new ones, and marvel at the recent restorations and accomplishments achieved through the Conservancy's efforts in the past six years. We invite you to become members of the Conservancy and

join us in helping to keep the Park as beautiful as you see it here in the pages of this book. Enjoy *Seeing Central Park* both at home and as the best guide for a visit to the Park itself. Either way, we promise you it'll be a walk in the park!

Douglas Blonsky
President of the
Central Park Conservancy
and Central Park Administrator

Central Park is one of the most important works of art in America.

Almost entirely man-made and built between the years 1858 and 1873, its visionary designers, Frederick Law Olmsted and Calvert Vaux, referred to their creation as "a single work of art." Composed of natural elements—turf, wood, water, and rock—and balanced with exceptional examples from the decorative and fine arts, the Park could also be perceived as an outdoor museum that brilliantly combines the kinds of attractions in its neighboring cultural institutions, the American Museum of Natural History and the Metropolitan Museum of Art. It is the intention of this book to guide both Park visitors and armchair travelers through this unique masterpiece and "museum without walls," interpreting and explaining—through words and images—how to see Central Park.

INTRODUCTION

Contrary to Lee Lorenz's delightful *New Yorker* cartoon, Central Park is America's first theme park, and its "theme" is Nature. Many people assume that the 843-acre Park is a slice of the last remaining virgin territory on Manhattan Island, but nothing could be further from the truth. When the site was set aside in 1853 for a future park in New York—two and a half miles north of the city's center—1,600 people lived on the scruffy and "broken," landscape. In most places only three or four inches of soil lay between the surface and the bedrock below. Inhabitants of the small communities that lived on this land worked hard to wrest small kitchen gardens and a few fruit trees from the barren terrain, jagged cliffs, polluted swamps, and noxious fumes—by-products of the area's bone-boiling factories, pigsties, and slaughterhouses.[1]

VICTORIAN DESIGN: THE ROMANTIC LANDSCAPE

As with contemporary theme parks, the natural and manufactured elements that make up Central Park were planned, planted, and placed according to the practical and aesthetic decisions of its designers, Frederick Law Olmsted and Calvert Vaux, who won the design competition for Central Park in 1858. For the next sixteen years the designers and their team of more than 4,000 laborers, gardeners, stone masons, engineers, and artisans blasted rock, drained swamps, moved tons of earth, and built roads, walks, and ornamental structures. The result—unlike the commercial theme park referenced in the cartoon—became one of America's most important and enduring works of art whose man-made greensward and gardens, woodlands and water bodies, bridges and byways sought to evoke the idealized scenes painted by contemporary artists of the Hudson River School.

"When they built this, Jeremy, parks didn't have themes."

The Lake

In the decade preceding the construction of the Park, America's first school of painting emerged in the scenic Hudson River Valley, north of New York City. Such painters as Thomas Cole, Asher Durand, and Frederic Church celebrated on canvas the nation's natural landscapes, ranging from such awesome scenic wonders as Niagara Falls to the more intimate woods, meadows, lakes, and streams of the Catskill Mountains and New England.

The Park's designers were closely connected with these paintings and with the natural scenes that inspired them. As a young boy, Olmsted, born in Connecticut, was trained by his father to admire the local landscape as they traveled on horseback and carriage. In the early nineteenth century middle class Americans, like the Olmsteds, were discovering for the first time the leisure-time pleasures of scenic tourism, or sightseeing, as we call it today. Later in his life, Olmsted traveled widely to visit the magnificently designed estate parks of the monarchs and aristocrats of Britain and continental Europe. In England he was especially excited and inspired by Birkenhead Park. Opened in 1847, it was the first free public park in the world to be created by a municipality, and it welcomed all citizens of Liverpool.

As a young architect, Calvert Vaux had taken many sightseeing and sketching trips through his native Britain and Europe as well. When he moved from London to the Hudson River Valley in 1850 to design private homes and estates for the well-to-do and growing middle class, he immediately fell in love with the varied landscapes of his newly adopted country. Vaux also fell in love with and married Mary McEntee, whose brother, Jervis McEntee, was a painter of the Hudson

River School. Thus his circle of professional colleagues and friends both upstate and in New York City, where he moved in 1856, included the leading landscape designers, artists, poets, and writers of the day, whose works of art celebrated America's unrivaled scenery.

When the time came to design Central Park, the newly formed partnership envisioned "a gallery of mental pictures"[2] more like those paintings they had admired and the scenery they had enjoyed on land-scaped estates. Thomas Cole, founder of the Hudson River School, explained that, for him, a landscape painting was an ideal assemblage of elements from the natural world. " . . . [t]he most lovely and perfect parts of Nature may be brought together, and combined in a whole that shall surpass in beauty and effect any picture painted from a single view."[3] Similarly, Olmsted theorized that "[a] mere imitation of nature, however successful, is not art." And it was most certainly art that he and Vaux aspired to in their design for Central Park. In the natural world it was, he explained, "unlikely that accident should bring together the best possible ideals of each separate [landscape and] still

Frederick Law Olmsted

Calvert Vaux

more unlikely that accident should group a number of these possible ideals in such a way that not only one or two but that all should be harmoniously related one to the other."[4] Thus, Central Park—like any great work of art—was intended to be greater than the sum of its individual parts, and Olmsted and Vaux said as much in their most famous statement, "[t]he Park throughout is a single work of art, and as subject to the primary law of every work of art, namely that it shall be framed upon a single, noble motive, to which the design of all its parts, in some more or less subtle way, shall be confluent and helpful."[5]

AN ELEGANT TAPESTRY

The design of the Park is simple and elegant, a beautiful tapestry made up of three types of landscapes—the pastoral, the picturesque, and the formal—that have three distinct modes of transportation—carriage drives, bridle paths, and pedestrian paths—threading their way through constantly changing scenery.

The **pastoral landscape** takes its name from the Latin pastor or "shepherd who grazed his flock in a large open meadow or pasture." When Olmsted and Vaux designed their plan, they named it "Greensward," the English term for a vast lawn dotted with small clusters of shade trees—the type of landscape they most wanted for Central Park. The designers understood that creating seemingly limitless meadows and

expansive lakes would best solve the problem of how to create the illusion of a rural landscape within the rigid rectangle of parkland, carved from Manhattan's gridded streetscape. The edges of the meadows were designed to be irregular and indistinct so that the play of sunshine and shadow would hint at a sense of infinite space. The designers wanted "[a] broad stretch of slightly undulating turf without defined edge, its turf lost in a haze of the shadows of scattered trees under the branches of which the eye would range . . . a space free of all ordinary urban conditions . . . [and] an encouragement to extend these purely rural conditions indefinitely."[6]

Water was also expected to contribute to the same visual expression of infinity as the meadows. As Vaux explained, "50 feet of water will give an idea of distance and of difficulty in passing it greater than 500 feet of ground will."[7]

Just as the broad meadows and lakes were intended to be the physical antidote for the uneven, "broken" landscape, so, too, were they created to be the psychological antidote to the "bent" mind. The Park's main purpose was to be a soothing and therapeutic alternative to the visual and mental chaos of urban life, to "unbend the mind," as Olmsted called it. "We want a ground which people may easily go after their day's work is done, and where they may stroll for an hour, seeing, hearing, and feeling nothing of the bustle and jar of the streets, where they shall, in effect, find the city put far away from them." It was the pastoral landscapes that the designers felt would best provide the "tranquility and rest to the mind" for the weary city dweller. It is also important to remember that Central Park was being planned and constructed during the turbulent decades before and during the Civil War. The nation was being torn in two and a soothing sanctuary that could also give stability to a troubled populace was undoubtedly a consideration of the designers. Olmsted and Vaux would often cite the "green pastures and still waters" of the Twenty-third Psalm to "restoreth" one's soul, as a park's ultimate purpose.[8]

Today Sheep Meadow, Cedar Hill, East Meadow, the Great Hill, North Meadow, and the Great Lawn are the Park's best examples of the pastoral meadows. The Lake and the Harlem Meer are the most enduring examples of a broad sheet of water while the more intimate Pool, Pond, and Turtle Pond suggest that they are a cove or inlet of a larger lake just beyond view.

The **picturesque landscapes** in Central Park are the three woodlands: the Hallett Nature Sanctuary in the lower Park, the Ramble in mid-Park, and the Ravine and the North Woods of the upper Park. For the woodlands, Olmsted and his Superintendent of Planting, Austrian gardener Ignaz Pilat, wanted to suggest "the mystery, variety, and luxuriance of tropical scenery."[8] Desiring a "natural wild character" with the interplay of light and shade, they created compositions of tangled vines, ferns, shrubs, mosses, and flowers combined with bold and jagged outcrops. He also wanted to feature fallen logs, wildflower meadows, quiet streams, graceful cascades, rusticated stone arches, and shelters, bridges, benches and fencing made from unmilled tree branches, roots, and trunks. The woodland flora was intended to attract a wide range of fauna from butterflies to a multitude of native and migrating birds. The designers even created rustic bee hives and birdhouses, and peacocks gave a sense of the picturesque whimsy, further encouraging portions of the natural world to take up residence in the Park.

Sheep Meadow

The Ravine

The **formal landscapes** are the most obvious designed areas. Created with the ruler and the T-square, this type of landscape typically features geometric, often symmetrically shaped lawns and flower beds, rows of trees planted in parallel lines, and topiary trees that are more sculptural than natural. Water bodies frequently take circular or rectangular forms, and fountains, sculpture, and structures are the focal points in long and straight vistas. Versailles is the world's most famous example of the formal landscape.

The straight streets and long vistas of the city's unrelenting grid provide a sense of orientation and predictability. In contrast, the picturesque woodlands replace that sense of comfort, familiarity, and a lack of variety with a sense of mystery and adventure by the dense plantings, maze of twisted pathways, meandering waterways, and secret spaces that were intended to mimic an authentic wilderness experience. In the woods we can simultaneously have feelings of playful disorientation, adventure, and surprise. Changes in direction, which one experiences while wandering a maze of hidden pathways, often signal changes in mood—from the surprise of a waterfall and the delight of a rustic bridge, to apprehension from the obscurity and uncertainty of the Huddlestone Arch, assembled, as it is, without mortar between the massive overhead boulders.

Unlike the autocratic fantasyland of such monarchs as Louis XIV and Marie Antoinette, however, Central Park's formal spaces would accommodate the needs and expectations of a democratic society. Here everyone would be welcome to enter and participate. The Park would provide the opportunity for ordinary citizens to promenade, listen to beautiful music, and admire magnificent architecture, fountains, works of sculpture, and ornamental horticultural displays—a royal walkway for people from every walk of life.

In Central Park the formal spaces of the Mall, Conservatory Water, and Bethesda Terrace, "the Heart of the Park", stood apart from the rest of the Park's more naturalistic landscapes.[9] "[O]n general principles," the designers stated their "aversion to a symmetrical arrangement of trees," however, they considered a grand promenade "with elements of grandeur and magnificence" to be "an essential form [for] a metropolitan park."[10] These formal areas were to be discovered only after the visitor had experienced the more naturalistic pastoral landscape, such as the Pond, that greeted them as they passed through the Park's entranceways. Even architect Calvert Vaux dictated that "Nature [be] first, 2nd and 3rd, architecture after a while."[11]

A MOVING PICTURE GALLERY

In many respects, a visit to the Park is not unlike a trip through the Hudson River School painting galleries of the Metropolitan Museum of Art or the New York Historical Society. The viewer first admires, say, a bucolic scene of sheep grazing in a rolling meadow, then moves a few steps further to view another painting that captures dappled sunlight falling on a woodland waterfall, then on to a study of ferns, vines, and wildflowers growing from the crevices of a weathered rock outcrop. In much the same way, visitors to Central Park move from one composition to another. The board of commissioners commented in their 1861 annual report that "[t]he Park has attractions to those that visit it merely as a picture . . . the eye is gratified at the picture that constantly changes with the movement of the observer."[12]

THE PEDESTRIAN PATHS

The most interesting "passages of scenery" were designed to be experienced on foot. The original twenty-eight miles of pedestrian paths (now fifty-eight miles) vary in length, width, and variety. The Mall is the most prominent of the pedestrian paths, being both the widest and only straight promenade intentionally designed for the Park. At the north end is the Bethesda Terrace, which is the focal point of several converging paths. The paths in the Park often lead over or under one of the thirty-six ornamental bridges, which frame a view or offer a commanding overview of the landscape beyond. Several paths surprise visitors with a rustic shelter, positioned as a resting spot and viewing platform atop one of the Park's many prominent rock outcrops. The most intimate pathways wind through the Ramble and other woodlands, shutting out the rest of the Park until they gradually skirt the edge of the woods, often providing a glimpse of a meadow or a lake to tease the visitor's curiosity to continue on.

THE CARRIAGE DRIVES

Before Central Park was created, there were few opportunities in the city to ride through natural scenery either in a horse-drawn carriage or on horseback. The streets of New York were chaotic. The attractive shoreline vistas were inaccessible except on foot, and only rutted and muddy roads led to New York's more bucolic suburbs, such as Greenwich Village or Bloomingdale alongside the Hudson River, now the Upper West Side. In fact, very few affluent people even owned carriages before the Park was built as there was little opportunity for a pleasant ride in a country setting close to home. All that changed with the state-of-the-art drives and bridle paths of Central Park. The carriage trade expanded for the well-to-do, and vast numbers of stables were constructed near Park entrances for horseback riding on the bridle paths.

With few exceptions, Olmsted and Vaux swept the roadway in far from the four streets that form the Park perimeter to simulate a drive in the country. To further enhance the impression of a drive in the country, they planted a screen of tall trees and dense shrubbery both inside and outside of the Park's wall to obscure buildings from the eye of the Park visitor.

The Park's irregular terrain favored the construction of winding and curvilinear roads, discouraging the use of the drives or bridle paths for racing. According to the designers, "a beautiful open green space, in which quiet drives, rides, and strolls may be had . . . c[ould] not be preserved if a race-course, or a road that can readily be used as a race-course, is made one of its leading attractions."[13]

In the original Greensward plans, horsemen and vehicles were meant to travel on shared thoroughfares. Olmsted and Vaux had created a mere 1.5-mile loop around the upper Reservoir as the only discrete horseback "Ride" in the Park. But two influential commissioners made it very clear to the designers that they intended to ride roughshod over any concept that prevented horsemen from having a route of their own.

THE BRIDGES
OF CENTRAL PARK

Famous horseman and commissioner August Belmont (namesake of New York's Belmont Raceway and Belmont Stakes, and founder of the Jockey Club) and his colleague Robert Dillon complained that Olmsted and Vaux's bridle path was inadequate, and the designers were ordered to extend it throughout the already narrow landscape. Reluctant to remove even an inch of wood, water, or turf for an additional thoroughfare, the designers came up with a brilliant solution to the commissioners' demands: They created a system of bridle paths, pedestrian paths, and carriage drives, which were separated from each other. A series of ornamental arches and bridges allowed intersecting routes to pass over and under one another for the sake of public safety without sacrificing precious parkland.

Greywacke Arch

Riftstone Arch

THE TRANSVERSE ROADS

The separation of traffic—by carriage, horse, or foot—through the use of bridges inside the Park was actually an extension of the designers' most original and innovative aspect of the Greensward plan, a system of over- and underpasses outside the Park for the competition's requisite transverse roads—an idea that contributes greatly to isolating Park visitors from city traffic and maintaining the unity of the Park as "a single work of art."

Because the Park is two-and-a-half miles-long, the commissioners knew that one of the most important requirements in the design competition would be the inclusion of at least four east-west transverse roads that would cross the Park at regular intervals and be open to city traffic around the clock. Every design submission, except for the Greensward plan, put these roads on the same level as the Park landscape. The result would have divided the Park into five small, separate sections. The constant flow, noise, and fumes of traffic, which in the nineteenth century ranged from a horse-drawn fire engine to a herd of cows on their way to an east side slaughterhouse, would certainly have disrupted the sense of bucolic serenity within the Park.

The Greensward plan's innovative concept depressed those four transverse roads in trenches more than eight feet below the surface of the Park.

They were referred to as "sub-ways"—very possibly the first use of the term that has come to represent New York's famous underground transportation system. The designers' brilliant resolution unified their artfully designed landscapes by constructing bridges that carry the Park's drives and walkways over those four sunken roadways, camouflaging the sight and sound of commercial traffic with luxurious plantings. This innovative concept became the inspiration for the over- and underpasses of our modern highway system, a phenomenon that the designers of Central Park could never have imagined in their wildest dreams.

THE VICTORIAN PARK:
THE GRAND TOUR

The Park was created at a time when high fashion dictated that well-to-do Americans of the New World take the Grand Tour of the Old World. A visit to the ancient temples and ruins of Greece, the medieval cathedrals of Italy, the famous chateaux and gardens of France, and the exotic mosques and venerable relics of Moorish Spain and the Holy Land were de rigueur for Americans who jealously coveted the famous historic landmarks and ruins of Europe and the Near East. But for the average American, foreign travel was only a dream until the creation of Central Park, where exotic architecture and features could evoke the Grand Tour.

The designs in the Park were influenced by the 1851 international Crystal Palace exhibit in London and in New York (1853), where countries of the world assembled under one roof to display the finest works and traditions of their respective cultures. These exhibits gave mid-century Americans and Europeans, hungry for new and exotic information, the first-hand experience and exposure to paintings, sculpture, textiles, furniture, and clothing previously unknown, and at the same time, the new invention of photography, in the form of cheap stereographs, offered New Yorkers views of foreign architecture, landscapes, and peoples.

The Moorish-inspired fantasies of the Mineral Springs Pavilion, the Bandstand (right)—both now demolished—and the Minton Tile arcade; the Gothic-inspired Belvedere Castle, Dairy, and Sheepfold; and the Baroque design of the Bethesda Terrace gave Park visitors a taste of Europe and the Near East. The Dene summerhouse could trace its oriental designs to rustic structures in Chinese gardens. These ornamental structures, along with meadows that resembled England's green pastures, Versailles' grand allées and promenades, and America's indigenous groves and forests, and such attractions as a camel ride led by a zookeeper in an Arabian costume or a ride in an authentic Venetian gondola, all combined to shape a Central Park that was, in many respects, a theme park, a century and a half before Orlando's Epcot Center, where visitors are encouraged to "explore the world in a day."

The Bandstand, 1864

THE OUTDOOR MUSEUM:
VICTORIAN DECORATIVE ARTS

Another way to experience Central Park is to appreciate it as an outdoor museum of Victorian decorative art. The Park's structures were at the forefront of civic art and national public art and architecture. A walk through the Park reveals some of the finest ornamental buildings, bridges, fountains, and furniture that reflect the preeminent styles of mid-nineteenth-century America and Britain.

Calvert Vaux and his colleague and frequent collaborator Jacob Wrey Mould came of age just as the Gothic Revival became the most popular and accepted style of the day. Vaux spent his early years assisting architect Lewis Cottingham, a well-known practitioner of the Gothic style. John Ruskin, the British critic and a strong influence on Olmsted as well as Vaux and Mould, was the leading advocate of the Gothic style. Two of the Park's buildings—the Dairy and the Sheepfold—exemplify this popular style of architecture as do details of Trefoil, Inscope, Graystone, Dalehead, and Springbanks Arches and the magnificent cast-iron "Gothic" Bridge No. 28 at the north end of the Reservoir. Belvedere Castle was created in the earlier Norman Romanesque style of architecture. Bow Bridge, the oldest and largest span in the Park, features the cinquefoils so commonly found in Gothic tracery.

Bridge No. 27

Mould discovered his talent for the decorative arts while assisting the recognized genius of ornamental design, British architect Owen Jones. Mould possibly helped Jones with his encyclopedic masterwork, *The Grammar of Ornament*, a compilation of design elements from ancient, medieval, and modern eras in Western civilization as well as the Near East, Asia, and Africa. The book became the guiding force for all subsequent architects and designers, and Vaux and Mould were no exception. They would have absorbed Jones' design principles as well as appreciated the new and exciting vocabulary of ornamentation at their disposal.

Jones warned his readers that merely copying past styles would be "inappropriate," as it would never honestly reflect one's own time and place. "The principles discoverable in the works of art of the past belong to us, not so the results."[14] Vaux and Mould understood Jones' advice. True to the master's principles, Bethesda Terrace, the Bandstand, Mineral Springs

Bethesda Terrace, detail

Pavilion, Cherry Hill Fountain, and the ornamental bridges did not replicate any specific historic style, but rather became a blend of Italian Gothic, Celtic, and Arab-inspired designs of Moorish Spain. The designers adapted or merged historic decoration to form an entirely new and fresh ornamental approach for Central Park—and for America.

Owen Jones believed that ornament grew out of our desire to imitate forms of nature and, indeed, the both abstract and representational designs that Vaux and Mould created for their buildings and bridges celebrated the natural vegetation seen throughout the Park's landscapes. Vaux and Mould's elaborate stone carvings, richly ornamental cast-iron creations, and tile design were extremely advanced—an absolute first in American public architecture. Their groundbreaking designs of the 1860s were precursors to the Arts and Crafts movement as well as the architectural designs of Louis Sullivan and Frank Lloyd Wright.

A new style, that of rustic art and architecture, also made its first public appearance in America in Central Park. Furniture, bridges, fencing, and intimate summerhouses fashioned from unmilled tree trunks, branches, and roots originated in China and became popular by the eighteenth century on private estates in Britain. Tastemaker Andrew Jackson Downing had a few rustic seats and structures on his private property at Newburgh in the Hudson Valley where his young partner Calvert Vaux would have admired them on a daily basis. In the nineteenth century Central Park had more than one hundred rustic features mostly designed by Vaux, who earned a reputation for the originality of his fanciful architecture. Examples range from the Kinderberg, the largest and most elaborate summerhouse (now demolished), to elegant seats, fences, bridges, bird houses, and even bee hives in the Ramble.

Rusticated arches, created from blocks or boulders of undressed stones that were blasted from the Park's rock outcrops, are also some of the Park's most important decorative features. Notable are the Riftstone Arch over the west side bridle path, the Ravine's Huddlestone and Glen Span Arch, and the Ramble's Rustic Stone Arch.

THE MORAL LANDSCAPE: THE GATES

The commissioners of Central Park did not intend the Park entrances to exist as gaps in the perimeter wall as they are today. Instead, they envisioned gates that were modest in design and whose main function was to close the Park at midnight. When they could not agree on the design for the gates, they decided to postpone the decision—a decision that leaves us with today's empty spaces. What they did agree on, however, was the names of the gates, suggesting yet another theme for Central Park—the theme of Work.

In the report that explained the names of the gates, the Commissioners emphasized the importance of naming Park entrances so that visitors would have an "apt and convenient" way of arranging a meeting place. As they did not want people to reference the city's grid ("I'll meet you at Fifth Avenue and 72nd Street"), they created a system that celebrated New Yorkers for the hard work and productivity that led to the creation of the Park. "The construction of the Park," they wrote, "has been easily achieved, because the industrious population of New York has been wise enough to require it, and rich enough to pay for it." Thus the names of the gates along Fifty-Ninth Street were grouped into four main categories: Scholars (Fifth Avenue), Artists (Sixth Avenue), Artisans (Seventh Avenue) and Merchants (Eighth Avenue). They dedicated the remainder of the gates to past and present New York laborers: Pioneers, Farmers, Woodsmen, Miners, Mariners, Engineers, Inventors, Warriors (army and navy), Saints (religious workers), Strangers (immigrants who contribute to America's work force), Children (for their future place in the work force), and Women (notable, among other professional contributions, for their domestic services).[15]

Today the professions and groups have been recently inscribed in the walls at the eighteen original entrances, but it was the commissioners' intention to honor the professions by statues that would eventually flank the appropriately named gateways. Today the statue of

Samuel F. B. Morse at Inventors' Gate (at East 72nd Street) and Alexander von Humboldt at Naturalists' Gate (on West 77th Street) are the only two instances that exemplify the commissioners' original idea. Whether through inscriptions or statues, the commissioners intended each visitor to Central Park to be reminded that a Park visit was a reward that comes *only* to those who subscribe to the work ethic on which America was founded.

Bethesda Arcade, Minton tiles

AMERICA'S FIRST SCULPTURE PARK

In recent years the grounds of many public, private, and corporate sculpture collections have become venues for viewing works of art in the landscape, but Central Park is actually America's first sculpture park. The fountain at Bethesda Terrace, *Angel of the Waters* by Emma Stebbins, was the only work of sculpture commissioned for Central Park; officials assumed that other sculptures for the Terrace and the entrance gates would eventually be funded by private groups or individuals. The fifty-one bronze and marble statues scattered throughout the Park were gifts from various individuals or groups, who wished to donate works of art to Central Park or to memorialize in bronze or stone the great political or cultural figures of American and European history.

THE MODERN PARK:
A PARK ON THE GO

Over the course of its 150-year history, Central Park has always been a reflection of the most important values held by the society of the day. The nineteenth-century Park was created as an individual's oasis in the chaos and commotion of the city—a place for quiet contemplation and an appreciation for nature. In the twentieth century those important needs for escape continued for many; however, for the most part, the next generation of New Yorkers preferred outdoor communal gatherings that echoed the hustle and bustle of the new, electrified cityscape. At this time, New Yorkers created the nation's most famous amusement parks at Coney Island and the new sports stadiums of the Polo Grounds, Dodger and Yankee Stadiums, as well as small local parks, playgrounds, and recreational facilities.

As a result of these changing priorities, roughly one-third of the Park's original design was altered to reflect those new recreational interests. Between the years 1926 and 1966, twenty-one playgrounds, Wollman Rink, Lasker Rink and Swimming Pool, the Tennis House and tennis courts, North Meadow, and Heckscher and Great Lawn Ballfields were built in the Park. The new Park recreation specialists developed popular recreational, sports, and cultural programs that attracted a different energy and audience to Olmsted and Vaux's pastoral ideal.

When Model Ts, Packards, and Studebakers replaced fancy horse drawn carriages, many pedestrian gates were transformed into vehicular entrances. Olmsted and Vaux's curvilinear drives were either straightened or removed entirely to make life easier for the new suburban commuter. Parking lots, traffic lights, and traffic signs brought the hustle of city life into the once bucolic retreat. Whereas the former carriages moved clockwise through the Park, the automobile drives were reconfigured to go counterclockwise, radically changing the way many Park visitors experienced Olmsted and Vaux's scenery.

Whereas the designers felt that the Park in and of itself was the City's most important cultural institution, many acres of landscape were gradually given over to new, cultural features. Park architects Jacob Wrey Mould and Calvert Vaux designed the original buildings for both the American Museum of Natural History and the Metropolitan Museum of Art. The invention of electricity brought nightlife to Central Park. Walkways and buildings formerly dark after sunset brought new programs and new audiences to the Park. In 1923 Mould's cast-iron Bandstand and surrounding fountains on the Mall were replaced by a state-of-the-art Bandshell and not only classical but also popular music and jazz were performed in the Park. Adjacent to the Bandshell, the Vaux-designed Casino, a sedate Victorian restaurant, originally intended for "Ladies," was renovated by the celebrated Art Deco master Joseph Urban to become a nightclub for the city's beau monde during the Prohibition era.

After the death of Vaux (1895) and Olmsted (1903), Central Park began a slow and steady decline. Samuel Parsons, the Parks Department landscape architect and Vaux's able successor, was constantly challenged in his fight to save the Park from politicians and opportunists, who threatened to encroach on precious parkland and who cared little for neither responsible management nor necessary maintenance. The Park in the 1920s experienced its first serious decline.

THE MOSES ERA

During the depths of the Depression in the 1930s, Commissioner Moses brought new life and new energy to the Park. He secured federal money and returned good maintenance and groundskeeping practices to the eroded landscapes, though he changed much of the original "look" of the Victorian Park when he demolished many of Vaux's most charming features. Almost all the decorative materials, textures, and colors that gave Central Park its interesting variety—marble, variegated granite, cast-iron, rusticated wood and stone, and polychrome paint—were replaced by the repeated use of red brick for all new buildings. Furthermore, many of the new facilities, such as the Delacorte Theater, Lasker Rink, and Pool and Loeb Boathouse, were constructed on sites that destroyed some of Olmsted and Vaux's most important views.

On a positive note, Moses orchestrated public programs for huge masses of school children and adults alike, from yo-yo boys to go-go girls, bringing free, popular entertainment to a public in the throes of economic hardship with such annual events as the Winter Carnival, square dance competitions, and the Harvest Moon Ballroom Dance Festival. The Commissioner turned the quaint Swedish Cottage into a marionette theater and the former Ruskinian Gothic sheepfold into Tavern on the Green restaurant without destroying their architectural integrity.

Post World War II became a new era of enchantment and popular entertainment to the Park's youngest visitors, America's first generation of television watchers. Influenced perhaps by E. B. White's 1945 children's classic *Stuart Little*, the story of a mouse who sailed his ship in the Conservatory Water, the area became a new children's district, introducing the delightful sculptures of *Alice in Wonderland* and *Hans Christian Anderson*, the Kerbs Boathouse and concessions, the Delacorte Musical Clock and the Central Park Zoo. Joseph Papp's free Shakespearean performances of the 1950s at the edge of the Great Lawn became so popular that the Delacorte Theater, evoking Shakespeare's Globe Theater, was constructed in 1962. And following the popularity of Disneyland, the Children's Zoo opened in 1961, a petting zoo and storybook animal farm featuring a giant concrete powder-blue whale and colorful Noah's Ark (now demolished). Central Park did, at last, feature a modern theme park.

ENDING THE CYCLES OF DECLINE AND RESTORE

The Moses Administration brought management, maintenance, and programming to the Park, but when the Commissioner left office in 1960 neither funds nor management plans were put into place, and the Park began a second, serious downward spiral once again. In the following decades Central Park became the stage for popular mass events that brought both new energy and new erosion to the hundred-year-old Park. Central Park was declared a National Historic Landmark in 1965 and New York City's first Scenic Landmark in 1974, yet that was not enough to ensure the proper stewardship and maintenance that it desperately needed. With severe cutbacks in the city budget and no leadership or accountability, the Park became an unsightly and lawless ruin. One of the most important national treasures had become a national disgrace.

Influenced by the global environmental movement that emerged in 1970s, many activists and concerned New Yorkers banded together to save 843 precious acres of the planet. In 1979 Mayor Edward I. Koch and Parks Commissioner Gordon J. Davis appointed urban planner Elizabeth Barlow (now Rogers) to the newly established position of Central Park Administrator—to oversee the daily operations of the Park, a position that had not been filled for more than seventy years.

A year later, in 1980, Koch, Davis, and Barlow established a public-private partnership between the City of New York and the newly formed Central Park Conservancy. The Conservancy began to raise private monies to supplement the dwindling city budget, and gradually took on more management and maintenance responsibilities.[16] In 1998 and again in 2006, the City of New York signed an eight-year management contract with the Conservancy, recognizing its excellent work and high standards in both restoring and maintaining Central Park today and for its continued care for generations to come. Today, through the generosity of thousands of New Yorkers, Central Park is once again the greatest urban park in the world, bringing joy to those who visit either once a day or once in a lifetime.

Harlem Meer before restoration, 1979

Harlem Meer today

PART ONE

59TH TO 65TH STREETS

① GRAND ARMY PLAZA

The Park's southeast corner was always considered its main entrance. Not wanting the area to feature any grand monument or major attraction, Olmsted and Vaux preferred a small plot of tree-lined turf for each side of 59th Street. By the turn of the twentieth century, however, the new philosophy of Beaux-Arts urbanism had taken hold in American cities, preferring the Parisian look of broad avenues, sweeping vistas, and plazas featuring grand fountains and gilded monuments.

In 1899 Karl Bitter, an Austrian-born architectural sculptor, proposed a plaza and fountain that was similar to the Place de la Concorde in Paris. Twelve years later the journalist and publisher Joseph Pulitzer left $50,000 in his will to build the Bitter-designed symmetrically arranged, horseshoe-shaped plazas on 59th Street. Situated in the southern plaza is the elaborate Pulitzer Fountain, which is topped by Pomona, the Roman goddess of abundance, who symbolized the opulence and prosperity of the Gilded Age.

SHERMAN MONUMENT

After his victorious performance in the Civil War, General Sherman moved to New York and made daily visits to the Park in his carriage. When famed sculptor Augustus Saint-Gaudens was a young boy, he idolized the general, so when the artist found himself living in close proximity to his war-time hero, he begged him to sit for a portrait bust in 1888. This later became the head of the *Sherman Monument.*

When the General died, Saint-Gaudens was commissioned to do a large-scale work of Sherman for a site in Riverside Park near Grant's Tomb. When the Grant family learned that their famous relative would be upstaged by another Civil War general, they urged landscape architect Samuel Parsons to find another location. Parsons recommended the *Sherman Monument* be placed at the intersection of Broadway and Seventh Avenue in Times Square, but Saint-Gaudens requested that it be placed in the middle of the Central Park Mall with the additional request that the Mall's precious elms be chopped down so as not to dwarf his masterpiece. Fortunately, Parsons talked him out of *that* idea in favor of the most coveted spot in Central Park, the tree-lined plaza at Fifty-Ninth Street.

The *Sherman Monument* became Saint-Gaudens' favorite of his many works of art over his lifetime. It is considered one of the artist's great masterpieces and, without question, it is the most significant sculpture in Central Park. The addition of a female Victory figure, modeled after several different women in the artist's life, adds complexity and innovation to the traditional war hero astride a horse.

THE POND

Olmsted and Vaux were given a dramatic canvas for the Park's opening act. The natural brook and lowlands of the original topography suggested a U-shaped water body, wrapped around a steep rock outcrop that they transformed into a leafy woodland slope. This abrupt juncture with the city provided urban dwellers with the immediate rural escape that the designers considered the most important function of the Park.

Originally the Pond featured ice skating during the winter season; however, the demand for additional attractions and entertainment gradually seeped its way into the culture of the Park, and the Pond became the site of a swan boat concession, the same iconic feature of the Boston Public Garden. The swan "velocipede boats," transported to Central Park in 1877, remained a popular feature until 1924.

In 1934, Park Commissioner Robert Moses closed the woodlands to the public, turned it into a nature sanctuary, and dedicated it to George Hallett (1895-1985), an active civic leader and an avid bird watcher.

CHILDREN'S DISTRICT
AND THE CAROUSEL

When the Central Park Commissioners drew up the list of features they required for the future park, there was no mention of structures or landscapes specifically targeted to children and their caregivers. Once the Park was opened to the public, however, the commissioners saw the need in the lower Park for a "Children's District," which would meet the recreational and practical needs of children, in particular underprivileged children, who often had to walk several miles just to reach the Park's 59th Street gates.

The first structure that Vaux designed was the Kinderberg—a Dutch word meaning "children's mountain"—an elaborate rustic summerhouse, specifically designed with small tables and chairs for young children. In the 1950s the Kinderberg was replaced with the Chess & Checkers House. Today it is a visitor center that also features game tables around the building's perimeter.

Olmsted and Vaux would never have promoted such a popular and commercial feature as a carousel, yet one was installed during a rival administration in 1871. Through a succession of either three or four different carousels over the course of its history, it has always been one of the most beloved attractions in the Park. Early carousels had no platforms; the animals probably hung on chains and flew outward due to centrifugal force, and the ride became known as "flying horses." They were often powered by pulling a rope or a crank. This early Central Park carousel is probably the one that is still pictured on every can of Dr. Brown's Black Cherry Soda.

When Olmsted and Vaux returned to power in 1873, they created a two-level structure, connected by a central pole. Below the platform, a live horse—some accounts also suggest the possibility of a mule—turned the central pole of the riders above. By the 1920s "horsepower" gave way to electric power and the Park's new carousel even featured a brass ring and an organ. When that carousel burned down in the 1950s, the Park acquired its present carousel, abandoned for years in a Coney Island storage depot. This carousel is a masterpiece of American folk art, created by the celebrated Russian carvers Solomon Stein and Harry Goldstein, who were noted for their unusually spirited and flamboyantly decorated horses.

THE DAIRY
AND WOLLMAN RINK

In 1928 banker and philanthropist William J. Wollman offered to erect a "Mother's Rest Center" in Central Park. He proposed that the building be staffed by professional nurses who would serve the needs of poor mothers and their children, who on hot summer days "don't dare go home [staying] in the park for hours and hours."[1] Ironically, invalids and their caregivers had been Olmsted and Vaux's intention when they envisioned the Dairy, which was to offer a quiet place for those in need. As construction of Calvert Vaux's gothic Dairy was being completed in 1870, however, the corrupt Tweed administration decided to turn it into what we could call today a "fast-food" restaurant,

which remained until it became a park maintenance shed sometime in the 1950s. Today Vaux's charming country cottage has been restored and serves as the Park Visitor Center and Gift Shop.

Though the Mother's Rest Center was never built, a member of the Wollman family did finally get to make a significant contribution to Central Park in 1951, when Kate Wollman, William's niece, dedicated the new Wollman Skating Rink to the memory of her parents and her uncles. Built on the northern arm of the former Pond, the rink is probably the most beloved of Commissioner Robert Moses' changes to the Park's original design.

HECKSCHER BALLFIELD

Different forms of ballgames were being played in American cities in the 1850s, but the form that eventually matured into baseball was then known only as "the New York game." It was developed in the 1840s by the Knickerbocker Club, a social club of mainly upper-middle-class members. Having no suitable place to play the game in New York, the men took the ferry across the Hudson to the Elysian Fields in Hoboken, where Alexander J. Cartwright first created the now familiar diamond-shaped field with the bases at four corners. In the design competition for the Park, the commissioners required each design to include three "playgrounds," the term for ball fields at the time.

Nonetheless Olmsted and Vaux's main agenda was for people to gaze upon green lawns, not necessarily to play on them. The designers wanted the landscapes in the Park to serve the greatest good for the greatest number of people, and they considered ball playing too specialized a use for the general public. The commissioners did, however, value the use of the park for educational purposes, so they rewarded school boys with good grades and good attendance the privilege of playing ball in the Park, though the lawns were only open a few hours a week for this purpose in order to protect the turf. Vaux designed the Ballplayers House as a comfort station for these young ball players. Girls were relegated to the East Green for croquet; co-ed sports simply weren't tolerated in polite society in the mid-1800s. Adults were not permitted to play baseball or cricket in Central Park until the 1920s. Rebuilt in 1990, the Ballplayers House now serves as a concession stand for players and spectators.

UMPIRE ROCK

Umpire Rock, one of the largest rock outcrops in the Park, was so named for its close proximity to the Park's "playground," where the new game of "base ball" was first played in the 1860s. The large outcrop functioned as a viewing platform for spectators in the same way that bleachers now provide seating for ardent fans—frequently the unofficial umpires of the game.

The rocks in the Park are made of Manhattan schist, the bedrock that anchors the iconic skyscrapers of New York City to the earth's crust. The schist was formed when shale, a sedimentary rock composed of clay and sand on the ocean's floor, was transformed under heat and pressure into a conglomeration of minerals, becoming metamorphic rock. Schist can be recognized by its glittering appearance, which is caused by flecks of imbedded white mica.

The rocks act as important design elements in the Park and are used as platforms for commanding views, stairways, informal seats for visitors, components in picturesque planting compositions, or as building blocks for such rustic bridges as Riftstone Arch, buildings such as Belvedere Castle, and picturesque fantasies such as the grotto at the Pool and the cave in the Ramble.

COPCOT

When Calvert Vaux designed the Copcot rustic summer-house, he could never have foreseen that it would one day have the city's modern skyline as a dramatic backdrop. Nonetheless, the shelter still provides visitors with an experience of rural life immediately upon entering the park and is a cool respite from the noise and heat on the city street below.

JOSÉ MARTÍ

It is pure coincidence that two monuments in Central Park, both located at 59th Street park entrances, should be memorials to the struggle for Cuba's independence from Spain: the *Maine Monument* and the dramatic bronze sculpture of Cuban poet and journalist José Martí, who was shot in battle fighting for his country's liberation. It was the tradition in Roman art to depict a horse rearing up to symbolize a hero who had died in battle. Artist Anna Hyatt Huntington com-

pleted *José Martí* in 1959, though due to the heated political climate in New York between pro- and anti-Castro forces, the statue wasn't dedicated until 1965, when the situation was less volatile.

Martí is accompanied by two other liberators of Latin America, *Simón Bolívar* and *José de San Martín*. In the 1950s, the three statues were appropriately placed in the plaza at the head of Sixth Avenue, which had been renamed Avenue of the Americas in 1945.

MAINE MONUMENT

When the warship USS *Maine* went down in Havana Harbor in 1898, Congress declared war on Spain for the liberation of Cuba, and four days after the disaster William Randolph Hearst's newspaper the *Morning Journal* began a fund to honor the fallen victims with a memorial. A site was selected—the same Times Square site that was rejected by Saint-Gaudens for his *Sherman Monument*. Unfortunately, due to a bureaucratic mix-up, a comfort station was built on the spot—today the TKTS ticket booth is there—and the hunt went on until the present site on Columbus Circle was chosen.

The figures on the lower monument were sculpted by Attilio Piccirilli and display allegorical figures of the Atlantic Ocean, the Pacific Ocean, Courage, Fortitude, War, Justice, and Peace. The gilded figures atop the monument are by architect Van Buren Magonigle; *Columbia Triumphant* in her seashell chariot pulled by three hippocampi (half-horse and half-seahorse) is said to be cast from the guns of the USS *Maine*.

THE ARSENAL

When visitors enter the Arsenal on Fifth Avenue they are surprised and delighted to see military drum lights and a pair of cast-iron cannon with rifles instead of the traditional newel posts and spindles on the main staircase. These 1930s additions as well as the original eagle and cannonballs over the doorway are reminders that today's headquarters for the New York City Department of Parks & Recreation was originally built as a New York State munitions depot in 1851.

When the fortress-like building was absorbed into the site for the new Central Park, Olmsted and Vaux used the building for their offices. The Arsenal also became the Park's first museum—a hodgepodge of assorted gifts to the Park: guns, paintings, skeletons, plaster casts of sculptures, and yes, even cages of live animals. The New York City weather station for the fledgling U.S. weather service began its home on the top floor, and from 1869 to 1877 the American Museum of Natural History had its first home in the basement. The wonderful WPA murals in the lobby by Allen Saalburg reflect the building's many uses, including scenes from the nineteenth-century Park, a frieze of Union soldiers, maps of parks, and a history of the Arsenal itself. The Greensward plan, Olmsted and Vaux's original entry to the design competition for Central Park, is in the conference room, viewable by appointment only.

THE ZOO (12)

When Central Park opened to the public in 1858, cities throughout the nation and Europe celebrated with an assortment of gifts: paintings, cannon, military medals, statues, and even live animals. No one ever planned on having a zoo—Olmsted and Vaux were dead set against it—but when the animals started arriving in droves, it became clear that something would have to be done. Philadelphians had already chartered a zoo, but New Yorkers beat them by default with the first public animal exhibits. No sour grapes for the City of Brotherly Love, however. Living up to their epithet, Philadelphia gave the Park one of its first gifts—a herd of fallow deer, which were sent to graze near the Mall and later to the site that would become the Metropolitan Museum of Art. When a Park messenger boy was the only available employee to care for a new bear cub, the commissioners realized they had better hire a more professional staff for their mushrooming collection of animals, soon to be known as the Menagerie. They made some room for cages in the basement of the Arsenal and in the area behind the building where the Central Park Zoo, the nation's first, has been located ever since.

In 1934 Robert Moses made the Zoo a permanent feature of Central Park, creating new buildings and decorating them with charming bas reliefs and bronze statues, such as *Dancing Bear* by Frederick George Richard Roth, the sculptor of the popular Balto statue.

DELACORTE CLOCK

Appropriate for a sculpture at the Zoo, the *Delacorte Clock* features a group of animal musicians—a bear with a tambourine, a goat with a horn, a penguin with a drum, a hippo with a violin, an elephant with an accordion, a mother and baby kangaroo with trumpets—that rotate every hour and half hour to nursery rhymes and popular tunes, while above them two monkeys strike the bell. The clock, designed by Italian sculptor Andrea Spadini and erected in 1965, was donated by philanthropist George Delacorte, who loved the medieval mechanical clocks popular for centuries in European squares.

PART TWO

65TH TO 72ND STREETS

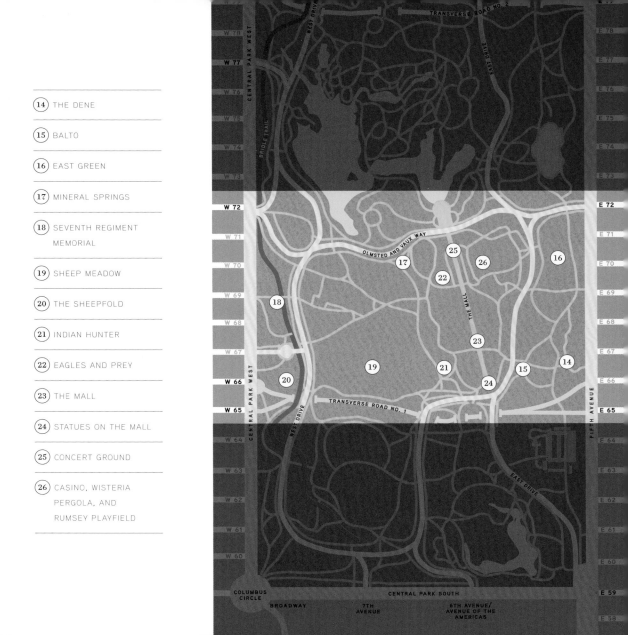

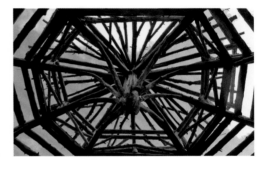

14

THE DENE

In the Dene, an English word for "valley," you can still appreciate the "broken" or undulating topography that characterized most of the pre-park landscape. Taking advantage of the high rock outcrop in the area, Vaux and his rustic craftsman Anton Gerstner created a quaint rustic summerhouse. Today the recently rebuilt shelter still enchants visitors while providing a dramatic contrast to the modern buildings now lining Fifth Avenue.

15

BALTO

Arguably the most popular sculpture in Central Park is that of Balto, the Alaskan husky who lead a relay team of dogsleds and their mushers to deliver a diphtheria anti-toxin serum to the people of Nome, Alaska, in February 1925. Ten months later the monument to Balto and his team was erected in Central Park, and Balto himself was there with his musher, Gunnar Kassen, for the dedication ceremony, making *Balto* the only effigy in Central Park to have had the honoree present at the unveiling. According to at least one newspaper account, Balto paid no attention to the speakers and tried to pick a fight with another dog.[1] The real Balto is stuffed and mounted in the Cleveland Museum of Natural History.

EAST GREEN

Once used as a croquet lawn for
girls, today the East Green features
some of the most beautiful flowering trees in the Park.

MINERAL SPRINGS

In the Annual Report of 1862, the commissioners noted with displeasure that "stands and refreshment houses, in which liquors are sold, have been placed on these sidewalks, so near to the [Park] entrances as to be not only very unsightly, but very objectionable."[2] To combat the saloons that were rapidly growing up near the Park, the commissioners approved the construction of a "Spring House," or "Mineral Springs" for dispensing mineral waters to park visitors. "Taking the waters," a panacea for almost any illness in the nineteenth century, was serious business. In the same way that we take aspirin or anti-depressants, nineteenth-century Americans and Europeans imbibed specific mineral waters deemed a curative for a vast number of mental or physical ailments.

By 1867 the Commissioners of the Park had given Carl Schultz and his partner permission to set up a concession west of the Concert Ground. Vaux designed a Venetian-Moorish fantasy to rival the spas and cafes of Europe, and possibly to also rival, intentionally or unintentionally, the nearby ornate and colorful bandstand designed by his colleague Jacob Wrey Mould. The interior featured marble panels and flooring with marble counters and silver faucets that dispensed the waters at five and ten cents a glass, which is comparable to the high prices for today's designer waters. The building, demolished in the 1950s, has been replaced with the Sheep Meadow Café concession in a nearby location.

SEVENTH REGIMENT MEMORIAL

Monuments of Civil War soldiers are familiar sites in town squares and public parks throughout America. The memorial to New York City's Seventh Regiment by John Quincy Adams Ward, however, was one of the first prototypes for the ubiquitous subject. In an unprecedented act, Olmsted and Vaux—who opposed statues in the Park—worked with Ward to create a different kind of representation—that of a watchful citizen-soldier, rather than the equestrian war heroes so often depicted throughout the history of art. The model for the statue, actor Steele McKaye, was also Ward's model for his *Shakespeare* on the Mall.

Sheep Meadow, early 1930s

SHEEP MEADOW

In the Sixties, Sheep Meadow became the iconic gathering spot for New York's counter-culture, the site of anti-Vietnam War protests, draft card burnings, peace rallies, Earth Day celebrations, love-ins, be-ins, and popular concerts. Originally a rocky and swampy terrain, the designers transformed the landscape into a pastoral meadow by blasting the outcrops and adding four feet of soil to the fifteen-acre site. It became the most expensive landscape in the Park to construct and the best example in today's Park of the designers' original pastoral vision.

Sunbathing, picnicking, or tossing a Frisbee—all popular activities on the meadow today—would have been frowned upon by Olmsted, who wanted park visitors to receive calming and refreshing thoughts by just looking at the greensward, not necessarily walking on it. Called "the Green" or "the Commons," the lawn received visitors only when signs were posted.

The name "Sheep Meadow" was established in the early twentieth century by Park visitors who had grown accustomed to the everpresent flock of pedigree Southdown (and later Dorset) sheep that had been grazing on the meadow for fifty years. In the 1960s the meadow became a popular stage for mass school programs, concerts, and events, but after decades of misuse and mismanagement, the meadow had become an unhealthy and unsightly dustbowl. Clouds of dust from the meadow choked the celebrants of the first Earth Day in 1970.

Under the care of the newly formed public-private partnership between the City of New York and the Central Park Conservancy, a restored and managed Sheep Meadow (1980) became an immediate success, sparking passion and inspiration among New Yorkers—many of whom had never seen a green lawn in Central Park in their lifetime—to restore all 843 acres of Central Park.

THE SHEEPFOLD

When a flock of Southdown sheep was donated to the Park in 1864, it was the perfect solution for mowing and fertilizing the lawn of what would come to be known as Sheep Meadow, not to mention a nice romantic touch that greatly appealed to Olmsted and Vaux. In 1870 Jacob Wrey Mould was asked to design an elaborate U-shaped sheepfold at the edge of the Green for the Park shepherd and his flock. The building Mould designed now houses a world-class restaurant, but fortunately, details of Mould's Victorian masterpiece have been preserved and can still be seen on the exterior of the building. The style that came to be called "Ruskinian Gothic," after British artist and critic John Ruskin, features wonderful contrasts of texture and color in the deep red brick, the blue-gray granite, and multicolored encaustic tiles.

INDIAN HUNTER

John Quincy Adams Ward's first sculpture, *Indian Hunter*, was considered a major breakthrough in American sculpture from the previous generation of classically influenced statues, such as the nearby *Angel of the Waters* by Emma Stebbins. Though Ward based the stance of his Indian on that of the famous ancient Roman *Borghese Gladiator*, he introduced real-life observation, even spending time with the Dakota tribe, to capture this truly American subject.

After a lifetime of sculpting both real life and symbolic personalities, including three works in Central Park, Ward reflected that his favorite theme was "nature and freedom," the subject of *Indian Hunter*. It is for that reason that the artist chose a life-size copy of this most cherished work for his own grave marker in Urbana, Ohio.

EAGLES AND PREY

Eagles and Prey, created in 1850 by French artist Christophe Fratin, has the distinction of being the oldest sculpture in the Park. Fratin showed a particular affinity for sculpting predators in the act of killing their prey, which, for a world about to be introduced to Darwin's radical theory of natural selection, was a startling new artistic viewpoint. Here the artist presents two eagles savagely staking a claim on their next meal—a goat, caught between two rocks. The protruding tongue and bulging eyes of the unfortunate animal adds a gruesome touch. Critics with a refined sensibility thought such violent art out of tune with the uplifting and spiritual nature of the Park. New Yorkers would have seen in Fratin's sculpture a witty reference to goats. At the time the city was overrun with goats, dogs, and pigs—the only solution to the garbage problem before the Department of Sanitation was founded in 1866. (Gotham, New York's well-known epithet, actually means "goat-town" in old English.) The commissioners' early reports complained that the trees in the Park were being eaten by wild goats, so when the commissioners were required to site this sculpture, they might have placed it near the Mall as a talisman to protect the precious elm trees.

THE MALL

The old English game, pall-mall, was played on a long, straight path with a ball ("pall") and a mallet ("mall"). Eventually the word "mall" came to mean a long, straight path lined with trees. When Olmsted and Vaux planned the design for the future Park, they knew a formal promenade would be one of its important features. Indeed today's Mall, lined with the third planting of a quadruple row of American elms, is the most important horticultural attraction in Central Park, the anchor of the design for the lower Park, and the core of the Park's democratic values.

If visiting the Mall evokes something akin to a religious experience, it is not coincidental. This planting of stately elms along a wide avenue was commonly known as a "cathedral walk,"

a design revered as America's rival to the famous gothic cathedrals of Europe. Olmsted spent much of his youth on elm-lined Temple Street in New Haven, Connecticut, so named for its similarity to an ecclesiastical structure. To Central Park, he brought his childhood memories, which are manifested in this quarter-mile procession of American elms whose arabesque and intertwined branches resemble the vaulting of a cathedral, and whose trunks resemble the columns marching down a nave. The golden light streaming through the trees, particularly early and late in the day, suggests stained glass windows, and the sculptures of poets and writers—known informally as Literary Walk or Poet's Walk—can be likened to side chapels dedicated to venerated figures.

The Mall is, in many ways, the defining feature of Central Park's democratic experiment. Before the Park was built, many doubted that people representing different races, religions, nationalities, and socio-economic groups would come together to enjoy a single public space. Yet others assumed that even if all groups did visit the Park, the wealthy and middle-class would seclude themselves in their private carriages or on horseback, never mixing with the less privileged pedestrians, who were "relegated" to the foot paths. Olmsted and Vaux saw this separation of classes on the city streets, so they designed the Mall and the Terrace—the Park's best walkways—to be the

central features of the lower Park. Only pedestrians could experience this magnificent walkway or stroll along the richly ornamented terrace and arcade. Expanding the philosophy to the entire Park design, an 1864 guidebook to the Park commented that "faithful to the pure democracy of [the designers'] doctrines, the best most varied and most numerous views lie along the path of the walkers."[3]

Today the Mall and the elm-lined Park perimeter on Fifth Avenue constitute the largest remaining stand of American elms on the continent. Dutch elm disease arrived in North America in the 1930s and destroyed many of the magnificent alleés that were so prevalent in cityscapes throughout America. Today, the tree crew of the Central Park Conservancy diligently monitors the trees and replants with young elms when the disease wreaks its havoc, ensuring that the Mall will remain a living memorial to this uniquely American landscape.

24

STATUES
ON THE MALL

In 1872, *Shakespeare* (right), by noted American artist John Quincy Adams Ward, was the first sculpture placed on the Mall. After *Sir Walter Scott* and *Robert Burns* arrived in the 1880s, the informal tradition of calling this section of the Mall Literary Walk or Poet's Walk began. Olmsted and Vaux were not pleased about having statues in the Park, despite their popularity with the public, so the designers instituted a strict policy requiring that all proposed sculptures must first receive approval by professional art organizations, that the site of the statue would be determined by park officials only after its acceptance, and that the work must commemorate men or women who have been dead for at least five years. Despite the ruling, there was a proliferation of statues in the Park.

Fitz-Greene Halleck (above) was the first sculpture in the city to commemorate a poet and the first sculpture of an American in Central Park. Today an all-but-forgotten figure, Halleck was the social wit and cultural leader of New York society in the mid-nineteenth century, and when the statue was unveiled in 1877 by President Rutherford B. Hayes and his entire cabinet, more than 10,000 people were there to celebrate Halleck's memory.

25

CONCERT GROUND

At the northern end of the Mall, we come to the Concert Ground, or the "choir loft" in the "cathedral's" transept, to continue the ecclesiastical metaphor. Today the 1923 Beaux-Arts concrete bandshell looms over the area, but in 1862 Jacob Wrey Mould created a more intimate and colorful cast-iron structure, the Bandstand, originally sited where *Beethoven* stands today. Mould, a dazzling and flamboyant character, was not only a gifted architect but also a talented musician who wrote lyrics and translated opera libretti. The cast-iron structure of the Bandstand perfectly married his passion for music with his passion for color. The structure itself was decorated with a symphony of more than twenty colors and was inscribed with the names of Europe's most famous composers.

As the popularity of the concerts at the Bandstand grew, so many visitors crowded the area that damage was caused to the roots of the young elms. Cleverly, Vaux designed attractive benches—reconstructed in the 1990s—that act as fences to protect the trees, while also providing seats for concert-goers.

Music wasn't the only sound heard on the Concert Ground—the chirping of live birds in gilded cages, which were designed by Mould, filled the air and were housed adjacent to the piers that featured a sculpted owl and rooster. Calvert Vaux, who had been awarded the book entitled *The Architecture of Birds* when he was an architecture student, cherished the book throughout his life and may have suggested the presence of both real and sculpted birds throughout the park. The four piers, created by Mould for Bethesda Terrace, feature stone birds in all seasons, while real peacocks, pea hens, and guinea hens roamed the woodlands of the nearby Ramble. The park commissioners began to

release birds over the park, and rustic birdhouses sheltered the many migrating birds that flocked to the newly built park. There were also stuffed birds in the basement of the Arsenal, the first home of the American Museum of Natural History as well as stuffed birds that were the rage of the Victorian era, prominently decorating the most fashionable women's hats. Today more than 270 birds can be viewed in the Park at various times during the year.

The Falconer (left) by George Blackall Simonds, a British sculptor and falconer, is sited on an outcrop to the west of the Concert Ground overlooking Olmsted & Vaux Way. It was installed in 1875, and celebrates the passion that New Yorkers have for the Park's rare birds of prey, such as the red-tailed hawks that have recently come to roost on the tall buildings surrounding the Park.

The statues of German composer Ludwig van Beethoven and poet Friedrich von Schiller grace the west side of the Concert Ground. Statues such as these were donated by newly arriving immigrants who wanted to celebrate the cultural heritage of their native country in their new home. These gifts to Central Park symbolize America as the great melting pot.

CASINO, WISTERIA PERGOLA, AND RUMSEY PLAYFIELD

In the nineteenth century, it was unthinkable for a proper Victorian woman, either by herself or with another female companion, to patronize a restaurant that catered to mixed company. Wishing to create a welcoming and protected environment for women, the commissioners had Calvert Vaux design the Casino, a Ladies' Refreshment Salon on a high plateau overlooking the Concert Ground. Visitors could also sit in the shade of the Wisteria Pergola, and listen to the free music concerts below. In the 1920s Vaux's simple hostelry was replaced with a crystal and gold nightclub for New York's beau monde, created by the world famous Art Deco designer Joseph Urban. A few years later, when Robert Moses became the Park Commissioner, the fashionable playground for the social elite was razed and turned into a playground for children, the Mary Harriman Rumsey Playground. By the late 1970s the playground was derelict and infrequently used. The Central Park Conservancy restored it as Rumsey Playfield in 1985, a sports area for school groups and the site of the popular SummerStage concert and performance series.

PART THREE

72ND TO 79TH STREETS

BETHESDA TERRACE

Bethesda Terrace, considered by Calvert Vaux to be the most important architectural achievement of his distinguished career, is never mentioned by scholars as a significant work of either American architecture or American decorative arts. Yet, with the exception of the Capitol building in Washington, few structures built in mid-nineteenth-century America rival Calvert Vaux and Jacob Wrey Mould's groundbreaking masterpiece. Passed over as a work of architecture, possibly because it lacks a traditional roof, the Terrace could be considered an intricate building on three levels with a complex and important decorative program unprecedented in any contemporary work of public art.

If the Mall is the nave of a majestic cathedral and the Concert Ground its transept, then Bethesda Terrace can be likened to the apse of this cathedral with its central fountain, *Angel of the Waters*, as its high altar. And like a medieval cathedral with religious themes carved into its facade, so too does Bethesda Terrace carry on this tradition with Vaux's sculptural program that equated nature with God—a common theme of both spiritual and popular thought in nineteenth-century America.[1]

The program for the Terrace begins at the end of the Concert Ground on the southern side of Olmsted & Vaux Way[2] with the first two sculptural piers representing the times of day: the Rooster of Day to the east and the Owl and Bat of Night to the west. The easternmost carving shows the rising sun and its floral symbol, a sunflower. Similar to a scene in a medieval illuminated manuscript, Mould's miniature wheat farm, now severely weathered, represents man's dependence on nature for his daily bread. The theme of work and the American work ethic, implied as one enters the Park's named entry gates, is reinforced once again as visitors descend the steps of their secular cathedral.

The companion scene on the Night pier represents one's evening work—reading and interpreting the Holy Word, here represented by an open Bible and a lamp, a sermon in stone to remind visitors that a trip to the park could also be a communion with God through his presence in nature. On the opposite side of that sacred still life, Mould carved a jack-o-lantern with a witch flying over the rooftops on a broomstick. Though there is no written account of what this humorous and

Spring

Summer

perplexing scene could represent, it may be a tribute to the pre-Christian Celtic peasant traditions that were still celebrated by the new Irish immigrants. The most important of their rituals—known today as Halloween, but originally the Celtic New Year, or *Samhain* (Gaelic for "summer's end" or "the setting of the sun")—marked the transition from summer to autumn and was appropriately placed to oppose the rising sun on the Day pier.

Vaux's comprehensive sculptural program for Bethesda Terrace called for many bronze and marble allegorical figures that were never created. Originally Vaux intended the four southern piers to act as pedestals for bronze figures depicting the four times of day, while directly across the drive statues of the Four Ages of Man and the Four Seasons of the Year on the staircases would have been connected such as Morning–Childhood and Spring and Night–Old Age and Winter. These themes, so common

Autumn

Winter

in the art and poetry of the nineteenth century, would have made Bethesda Terrace into the kind of "theme park" appreciated by the commissioners, who sought to impart moral lessons to every visitor to Central Park.

The sculptures on the Terrace represent a visual encyclopedia of botanical specimens in all seasons, and hardly a detail is repeated. The faithfully rendered fruit, flowers, plants, and birds on both the main panels and the four balustrades reveal Mould's talent for botanical illustration while the nonfigurative piers represent his ability to abstract and stylize vegetation, brilliantly foreshadowing the work of Louis Sullivan, the Art Noveau and Art Deco movements, and the botanical photographs of Karl Blossveldt.

28

BETHESDA ARCADE

Mould—who once remarked that he was "Hell on Color"—designed an elaborate tiled ceiling of more than 15,000 encaustic Minton tiles (the only instance in the world of a Minton-tiled ceiling), tiled flooring (now demolished), and either fresco or tile walls for the arcade's niches (never completed). His plan for the arcade transformed the potentially darkened crypt that connects the Mall with the open-air terrace into a shimmering jewel. Like a true eclectic, Mould's unique designs suggest, but do not copy, the colorful tiles of Moorish Spain, while his fanciful stone carvings combine elements from both ancient and modern decorative arts.

29

BETHESDA FOUNTAIN

In the movie *Fools Rush In*, New Yorker Alex Whitman (played by Matthew Perry) searches for one iconic symbol to sum up the magic of New York for his Mexican girlfriend Isabel Fuentes (Selma Hayak), and the one he invokes is the *Angel of the Waters* fountain: "There's a spot in the middle of Central Park," he says, "the Bethesda Fountain. If you sit there long enough the entire city walks by." Indeed, Bethesda Fountain is Manhattan's magnetic center. Just like the well was a gathering place in ancient Jerusalem or Rome, so this symbolic watering hole is the central assembly place in Central Park.

The celebrated fountains of Rome were undoubtedly the inspiration for sculptor Emma Stebbins—the first woman commissioned to do a public sculpture for New York City. Rome, the artist's home for fourteen years, had been famous since antiquity for the purity of its water system, and Stebbins dedicated her artwork to the healing powers of the pure Croton water that flowed from below the feet of her Biblical Angel.

When the statue was unveiled in 1873, the artist compared her *Angel of the Waters* to the angel in the gospel of John, who alighted on the pools of Bethesda and "made whole of whatever disease he had." A native New Yorker, Stebbins undoubtedly recalled the ravages of the deadly waterborne cholera epidemic of her youth, and years later would choose to celebrate "the blessed gift of pure, wholesome water, which to all the countless homes of this great city, comes like an angel visitant . . ." Stebbins identified the four smaller figures on the basin as emblematic of Temperance, Purity, Health, and Peace.[3]

30

CHERRY HILL AND WAGNER COVE

Cherry Hill, so named for the planting of cherry trees on the slope of the Lake, was originally a carriage turnaround, featuring an elaborate Victorian horse watering trough designed by Vaux and Mould. The six small cups on the fountain's main stem are drinking fountains for the many birds that visit Central Park. Wagner Cove on the western edge of Cherry Hill is one of the Lake's most intimate coves, featuring one of the Lake's six rustic boat landings.

Cherry Hill Fountain

31

THE LAKE

The illusion of infinite sheets of placid water lay at the heart of Olmsted and Vaux's pastoral park. It was so important to the designers that the Lake was the first landscape to be opened to the public in 1858. All of the Park's naturalistic water bodies, the Lake included, have a small, man-made island, an artistic and romantic touch that implies its creation by natural forces over time rather than by man.

In their original list of requisites for the 1858 design competition, the commissioners did not insist on the inclusion of water bodies for the future park. Their only requirement was to create an area that could be flooded over for winter ice skating. The popular winter sport had been previously unavailable to New Yorkers, as Manhattan Island lacked any natural ponds or lakes and the North (now Hudson) and East Rivers rarely froze. On December 19, 1858, only eight months after the announcement of the winning design, the man-made Lake was made available for skating—the unofficial "opening" of Central Park. Only 300 people skated that day, as most people did not own a pair of ice skates. However, many New Yorkers must have received ice skates as Christmas gifts, because more than 8,000 skaters were gliding on the ice on Christmas morning one year later.

Red flags or a red ball was hoisted from the top of the bell tower (later Belvedere Castle) to signal to New Yorkers that the ice was frozen for skating. A red ball was also displayed on the trolleys downtown to let New Yorkers there know that skating was available in the Park. In the evening hours, gas lamps would light up the ice for nighttime activities.

Boating was also a popular sport on the Lake. Originally there were three types of boats: two Venetian gondolas, private rowboats, and call boats for twelve passengers. These call boats would stop at each of the six boat landings, allowing visitors the opportunity to explore different areas of the Park. Today, visitors can rent rowboats and even an authentic Venetian gondola (powered by a gondolier) at the Loeb Boathouse on the easternmost shore of the Lake.

32

BOW BRIDGE

Many people are surprised that Bow Bridge, certainly one of the most iconic features of Central Park, was not in Olmsted and Vaux's original Greensward plan. Rather than construct a direct pathway to the Ramble, the designers wanted to offer visitors a slow and meandering pathway along the Lake's shoreline. However, two commissioners, Robert Dillon and August Belmont, were typically harried New Yorkers who insisted on a straight and direct shortcut to the Ramble. In response, the designers compromised by "throwing a light bridge" across the Lake "at as low a level possible." It quickly became a symbol of the Park itself.[4] Bow Bridge, named for its subtle curve resembling both an archer's and a violinist's bow, is the largest span in the Park and the second oldest cast-iron bridge in America. Cast-iron, a relatively new material at the time, was prized by architects for its tensile strength and malleability, enabling the designers to create graceful lines and forms that Vaux and Mould sought for their intricate Victorian designs.

The bridge was designed with eight flower urns, a fitting transition between the urns on the formal landscapes of Bethesda Terrace and the Mall to its south and the wilder, more natural woodland Ramble to the north.

33

THE RAMBLE

The Ramble is one of the greatest landscape sequences ever created by Olmsted and Vaux, and the one that best evokes the sense of mystery, surprise, adventure, and discovery of our childhood imagination. A dark cave, secluded coves, secret stairways, quaint rustic features, a maze of twisted pathways, huge boulders atop steep rock walls, wild vegetation, and the sights and sounds of migrating birds are all features that are present in today's Ramble. In the nineteenth century, rustic beehives and birdhouses, exotic live peacocks, pheasant, and guinea hen were also features of this natural "theme park." Whether you begin to explore the Ramble from Bow Bridge, with its sprawling vista of the Lake; or Belvedere Castle, with the expansive panorama of the Great Lawn; or the hustle-bustle of the East or West Drives, the obscure and intimate scenery of the Ramble provides an immediate and dramatic contrast to any of those entry points.

Azalea Pond (right), an intimate water body, has native woodland plantings that suggest an "American garden" of azaleas, rhododendrons, and other native plants and shrubs.

The Cave (right), closed to the public since the 1920s, once allowed visitors to row up to the underground walkway and climb the staircase that is carved into the rock outcrop, or to pass through and out to a secret opening.

The Stone Arch (opposite) seems to emanate from the flanking rock outcrops. Its shape echoes the Natural Bridge of Virginia and may possibly be Vaux's sly reference to one of the nineteenth century's most popular natural attractions in America.

34

LADIES POND
AND LADIES PAVILION,
HERNSHEAD

Originally a secluded water body on the western arm of the Lake, Ladies Pond was created so women could skate privately, but by 1864 the commissioners noted that the secluded pond was "unfrequented," as many women—especially those women new to the sport of skating—preferred to use the main body of the Lake with a male companion (skating provided men and women the rare opportunity to hold hands in public).[5] The water was filled in during the 1920s and now features the woodland gardens of Naturalists' and Azalea Walks along the western bridle path—one of the best country walks in the Park. In the future, a portion of Ladies Pond will be restored to the area.

Hernshead, a promontory in the Lake near the former

Ladies Pond (presumably a shape similar to the head of a heron or "hern"), is the site of Ladies Pavilion, one of the most important Victorian structures in nineteenth-century American decorative arts. Designed by Jacob Wrey Mould in 1871, the blue and gilt pavilion features decorative hanging pendants that were originally meant to be hanging flower baskets.

STRAWBERRY FIELDS

This small, teardrop-shape piece of land is Central Park's living memorial to the life and work of legendary musician and poet John Lennon, who often walked here in this landscape across from his home in the Dakota Apartments on 72nd Street and Central Park West.

Designed in collaboration with Lennon's wife, Yoko Ono, landscape architect and Olmsted scholar Bruce Kelly created a miniature Central Park within the 2.5-acre site, which is actually the summit of a large rock outcrop. The formal element is a circle of benches surrounding the *Imagine* mosaic. The lawn, dotted with magnificent trees, represents the designers' pastoral vision, and the slope is surrounded by picturesque plantings and an intimate woodland path.

Strawberry Fields was created as an international garden of peace, and a plaque on the east-west pathway names 121 countries who wished to be remembered in the name of Lennon and Ono's commitment to world peace.

36

PILGRIM HILL

In the original plans for the Park, Olmsted frowned on using flowering trees, as he believed they would distract visitors from experiencing the infinite and expansive views that were important for city dwellers. Nonetheless, the groves of magnolias, crabapple, and cherry trees that have been planted since are some of the most beloved attractions in Central Park.

A stand of Yoshino cherry trees graces Pilgrim Hill, a knoll overlooking the East Drive and named Pilgrim Hill for the statue of a pilgrim by John Quincy Adams Ward, donated to the Park by the New England Society in 1885.

37

CONSERVATORY WATER

Though the Children's District in the Park was originally created in the southernmost section of the Park, today we would probably consider Conservatory Water—popularly called either the Model Boat Pond or Sailboat Pond—as the area that features the attractions most beloved by today's youngest visitors. In 1945, E. B. White's classic *Stuart Little*—the story of a mouse who sailed his ship, "the Wasp," on Conservatory Water—may have influenced Park Commissioner Robert Moses to site the *Hans Christian Anderson* statue, the *Alice in Wonderland* statue, and the Kerbs Boathouse and outdoor café to the area where children had been sailing their model yachts since the 1860s. Today children can rent a model boat and imagine Stuart at the helm of their ship.

A formal garden was one of the requirements in the 1858 design competition, and Olmsted and Vaux planned to place their garden as well as a greenhouse or conservatory on the site of the present Kerbs boat house and café. During the construction of the Park, however, they substituted a formal reflecting pool for the flower garden. Though the conservatory was never constructed, the pool still retains the name Conservatory Water.

ALICE IN WONDERLAND

Alice in Wonderland is certainly one of the most popular sculptures in Central Park, and was said by a *New York Times* reporter to be "a statue that draws children as hot toast does butter."[6] Every day hundreds of children are dwarfed by Alice's huge lap as she sits cross-legged on her giant mushroom—a reference to Alice's sudden and enormous growth in her Wonderland adventures.

Placed in the Park in 1959, *Alice* is the work of Castilian sculptor Jose De Creeft, a friend of Picasso, whose personal work was more abstract than his *Alice*. De Creeft reworked the figures, originally conceived by Fernando Texidor, for donor George Delacorte, whose late wife Margarita loved reading *Alice's Adventures in Wonderland* to their children. De Creeft cleverly made the Mad Hatter a caricature of Delacorte, while Alice is a mixture of the sculptor's daughter, Donna Maria, and the Alice depicted in John Tenniel's famous illustrations.

HANS CHRISTIAN ANDERSEN

Birds are fixtures in this small plaza west of Conservatory Water. In the nineteenth century, a small pool of water was first erected in this site, and in the center was *Boy with Swan*, a fountain that spouted a spray of water from a bird's beak. In 1926 the area was selected as a possible site for the *Burnett Fountain*, in which one of the figures holds a bowl that is intended as a birdbath. Finally in 1956 the beloved statue by Georg Lober, *Hans Christian Andersen*, was chosen for the site. The renowned story-teller is depicted reading his famous tale, "The Ugly Duckling," as an attentive little duck—revealed in the story to be a swan—listens at his feet. Today *Hans* is the popular gathering spot for the bird-watchers whose telescopes and binoculars are frequently focused on the Fifth Avenue building (with the flat roof) that has hosted the nest of the famous red-tail hawk, Pale Male, his mates, and their avian offspring. Lober also paid loving homage to *his* mate with a secret inscription in the palm of Hans' left hand: "In appreciation of the help and encouragement my wife Nellie has always given me affectionately, Georg, 1956."

STILL HUNT

Many a jogger has been surprised by Edward Kemeys' life-
size bronze panther that crouches
on a rock ledge overlooking the
East Drive, the perfect example
of how the site of a sculpture
is integral to the artwork itself.
Kemeys became a sculptor while
serving as an axe-man during
the early years of the Park's construction and took a passionate
interest in the zoo animals. His
fascination led him to become
the foremost American sculptor
of animals in his time.

41

CEDAR HILL

The best sledding hill in Central Park, the steep slope takes its name from the wall of evergreens that have been synonymous with this area since it was planted. Glade Arch connects Cedar Hill to the lower Park.

PART FOUR

79TH TO 96TH STREETS

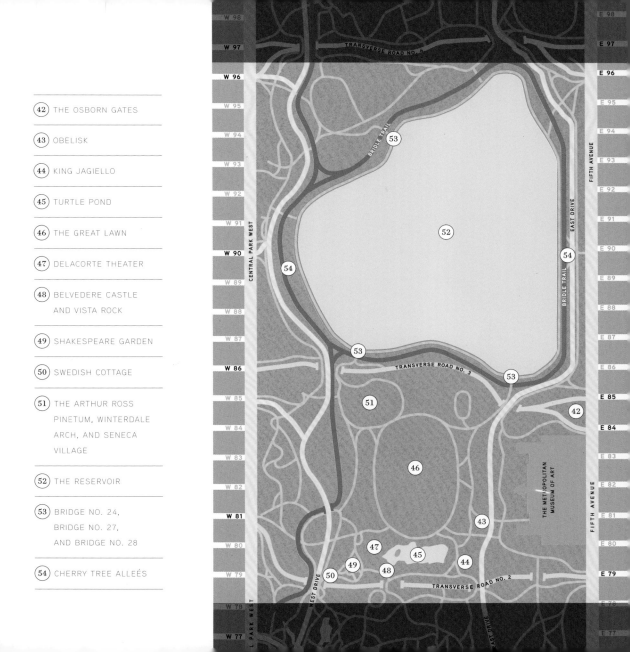

42

THE OSBORN GATES

In 1953 Paul Manship, the American sculptor best known for the *Prometheus* that looms over the skating rink at Rockefeller Center, won an award for the Osborn Gates as the best work of art for that year in New York City. The gates were placed at the entrance to the William Church Osborn Memorial Playground and dedicated to the former president of the Metropolitan Museum of Art. The gates were moved to the newly constructed Ancient Playground when the Temple of Dendur addition replaced the Osborn playground.

With its fanciful and decorative interchange of vegetation and animals, Manship chose to depict scenes from *Aesop's Fables* such as "The Crane and the Peacock," "The Tortoise and the Hare," and "The Fox and the Crow" (left). The artist enjoyed recycling his images in many different forms. *Group of Bears*, a statue of three bears, originally created in 1934 for the Paul Rainey Memorial Gates at the Bronx Zoo, appears three times within a three-block radius in Central Park: atop a pillar of the Osborn Gates, north of the Metropolitan Museum of Art; enlarged in the Pat Hoffman Friedman Playground, south of the Museum; and inside the Museum itself in the American Wing. Manship also created the animated bronze entrance gateway to the Tisch Children's Zoo in Central Park.

(43) OBELISK

When the magnificent grove of magnolia, crabapple, and flowering cherry trees surrounding the obelisk are in bloom, it becomes New York's version of the famous Washington Monument, the iconic obelisk in our nation's capital.

The Central Park Obelisk—Greek for "pointed instrument"—was one of a pair that had been carved from the rose-granite quarry at Aswan, Egypt, circa 1450 BCE, to honor the great warrior-king Pharaoh Thutmosis III. It had stood on the east bank of the Nile until 18 BCE, when it was moved to Alexandria during the reign of Caesar Augustus. The four corners of the shaft were chiseled away by local entrepreneurs, who had developed a business of selling pieces of the 71-foot, 244-ton stone to tourists and relic hunters. To steady the monument, the ancient Romans eventually placed four bronze crabs at the base of the obelisk—two of the original crabs are on display inside the museum; the crabs currently at the base are replicas, each weighing almost a ton, and were made in Brooklyn.

Park architect and designer Jacob Wrey Mould created the Egyptian style railings that surround the base of the monument, and in 1956 Cecil B. DeMille, the famous Hollywood director who had played near the obelisk in his youth, donated the money for the translation plaques. Its "sister" obelisk sits on the banks of the Thames in London.

KING
JAGIELLO

The equestrian statue by Stanislaw Kazimierz Ostrowski on the eastern shore of Turtle Pond commemorates King Wladyslaw Jagiello (pronounced yägye'lō), the first Christian Grand Duke of Lithuania who lead their Polish and Lithuanian forces against the Teutonic Knights of the Cross at the 1410 Battle of Grunewald. The statue was originally placed in front of the Polish pavilion at the 1939 New York World's Fair and remained in America throughout World War II. It was installed in Central Park after the war in 1945 as a testimony to the courage of the Polish people and the victims of the Holocaust. It is said that the King crossed the swords of his victims over his head as a sign of victory.

TURTLE POND

The small lake was named Turtle Pond by former Parks Commissioner Henry J. Stern in 1987 in honor of its reptilian residents. A nature blind has been added to the recent 1997 restoration of the pond so that park visitors might quietly observe the five species of turtles—red-eared sliders, snapping, painted, musk, and box turtles—as well as dragonflies, damselflies, and many varieties of waterfowl.

THE GREAT LAWN

In the 1830s New York City was under tremendous pressure to develop a pure water system for its citizens, who were dying from the lethal Asiatic cholera that eventually took the lives of more than 3,500 New Yorkers, or one in every fifty people. When the waterborne disease was traced to contaminated water contracted orally, it was decided in 1838 that damming up Westchester's Croton River, thirty-eight miles to the north, would be the best way to bring fresh water down through open channels, iron pipes, underground tunnels, and engineered aqueducts to homes and pump houses below 42nd Street. Today, New York City can claim to be "the world's oldest continuously running urban water supply."[1] The present Great Lawn is the site of the original fifty-five-acre York Hill receiving reservoir, whose water flowed through pipes (still under the Metropolitan Museum of Art) down Fifth Avenue to the distributing reservoir, on the site of today's New York Public Library and Bryant Park. A portion of the reservoir's northeastern wall can still be seen above the police precinct (originally the Park's stables) on the 86th Street Transverse Road.

When Olmsted and Vaux were designing the Park, they despised the reservoir's rectangular shape, an anathema to their vision for a curvilinear, romantic landscape. They camouflaged the massive stone walls with dense plantings and high earthen mounds.

When the old Croton system was rendered obsolete, the thirty-five-acre site was then left open to many proposals, among them a water lagoon, a memorial to soldiers in World War I, sports stadiums, airport landing pads, radio towers, a mausoleum for the storage of motion pictures, and a connecting road for cars and people from the American Museum of Natural History to the Metropolitan Museum of Art. The reservoir was finally drained in 1931 and filled with excavation material from Rockefeller Center and the Eighth Avenue subway. In 1937, a vast oval lawn and small playground areas opened to the public.

In 1979, when Sheep Meadow was under restoration, concerts and mass gatherings moved to the Great Lawn. Such great performers as Simon and Garfunkel; Diana Ross; Elton John; Dave Matthews; Bon Jovi; Luciano Pavarotti, Placidio Domingo, and José Carreras; the Metropolitan Opera; the New York Philharmonic; and religious leaders such as Pope John Paul II and Billy Graham, have all graced the Great Lawn. Unfortunately, those unrestricted sports, mass gatherings, and concerts left the once-green oval the "Great Dust Bowl." In 1995 the Great Lawn underwent an extensive and very costly two-year restoration by the Central Park Conservancy, and opened as a great, green oval that provides for both active sports and quiet contemplation.

DELACORTE THEATER

With a medieval castle as a fitting backdrop for many of the Bard's plays, entrepreneur Joseph Papp began to produce free public performances of Shakespeare's plays on the shores of Belvedere Lake (now Turtle Pond) in 1957. The free performances have become as synonymous with summer in Central Park as performances of the Metropolitan Opera and the New York Philharmonic on the adjacent Great Lawn. In 1962 philanthropist George Delacorte funded an outdoor theater, similar to the Bard's Globe Theater in London, which became the summer home of the Public Theater/New York Shakespeare Festival. The long lines for the free tickets are as legendary as the memorable performances themselves.

BELVEDERE CASTLE AND VISTA ROCK

48

In the same way that Hudson River School artists depicted a distant mountain peak in the background of their paintings, Olmsted and Vaux selected Vista Rock as the main visual attraction for visitors to the lower Park. They aligned the Mall and Bethesda Terrace with this prominent outcrop and placed Belvedere Castle on its summit.

The site of Vista Rock—so named by the Park's original engineer, Egbert Viele—features the most commanding views in this area of the Park, and the Belvedere, Italian for "beautiful view," reinforces the site's most significant function.

Just as designers of eighteenth-century private European parks created follies or "eye catchers," so, too, did architect Calvert Vaux create his own folly, a miniature Norman Gothic castle, to enchant visitors to Central Park.

Belvedere Castle was designed without doors and windows, as it was originally only meant to be a viewing platform. In 1919, however, the castle became the offices and instrument station for the U.S. Weather Service. Today weather readings are still taken from instruments at the top of the castle's tower as well as in a protective enclosure south of the castle and sent by computer to Brookhaven, Long Island. When you hear on a radio or television the words, "The weather in Central Park is . . ." you'll know that the weather report—often a bit of a folly itself—is being sent to you from New York City's most famous folly—Belvedere Castle.

49

SHAKESPEARE GARDEN

Dr. Edmond Bronk Southwick, a devoted reader of Shakespeare and the Parks Department's entomologist in 1886, developed a garden around the turn of the century at the request of Commissioner George Clausen, who felt that the nature library at Swedish Cottage should also have a neighboring demonstration garden. Slowly Professor Southwick began planting his "Garden of the Heart," which featured plants mentioned in the works of Shakespeare. In 1913, Commissioner Charles Stover officially named the tiny garden after the famous bard and in memory of his best friend and mentor, Mayor William Gaynor.

The lovely garden is miraculous, sitting as it is on Vista Rock's west side. With only a few feet of soil atop the rock's surface, the garden is nevertheless rich with shrubs and flowers mentioned in Shakespeare's plays and sonnets. Throughout the garden, small plaques feature Shakespearean quotes adjacent to related plants, such as "O how full of briars is this working-day world," (*As You Like It,* I, iii). Beside this is a bower of climbing roses—a reminder to stop and smell the roses, the purpose of both the garden and the Park.

SWEDISH COTTAGE

Originally known as the Swedish Schoolhouse, the Swedish Cottage came to America as Sweden's innovative entry to the 1876 Philadelphia Centennial Exhibition, a proud example of one of the first prefabricated buildings in the world. After the exhibition closed, the schoolhouse wound up in Central Park, purportedly the decision of Frederick Law Olmsted. Originally the building was used as a much-needed tool house, which may be the only explanation as to why Olmsted—who was dead-set against putting structures in the Park—allowed this structure. He must have appreciated its rustic charm.

Whether it was used as a maintenance building is not certain, though we do know that it was used at various times as a restroom (until the Swedish people complained), a tearoom, a shelter for cyclists, an entomology lab, and a nature library for children. During World War II the building was used as a civil defense shelter and finally, in 1939, Mayor LaGuardia turned the building into the charming children's marionette theater that it remains today. The late Shari Lewis (of Lambchop fame) learned her art from the first Swedish Cottage puppeteering staff.[2]

THE ARTHUR ROSS PINETUM, WINTERDALE ARCH, AND SENECA VILLAGE

Among the original features for Central Park, Olmsted and Vaux conceived of a Winter Drive, which they achieved by lining the West Drive from 72nd Street to 102nd Street with a collection of evergreens so visitors could enjoy the greenery from their horse-drawn sleighs. Recent plantings of pines on the West Drive at Winterdale Arch, the Arthur Ross Pinetum, and Strawberry Fields have slowly brought back the feeling of the Winter Drive to today's Park visitors, who are far more likely to enjoy the snow-covered landscapes on a pair of cross-country skis.

The Arthur Ross Pinetum (right) began very modestly when in 1971 Arthur Ross, a concerned citizen, philanthropist, and a passionate lover of pine trees, was disturbed that the maintenance buildings on the 86th Street Transverse Road ruined pastoral views from the Great Lawn. Ross, who had business experience in the pulp and paper industry, funded the planting of pines in the northern area of the Great Lawn oval.

Today those Himalayan pines are thirty feet high and the Pinetum's collection has grown to sixteen species, and stretches as far east as the Metropolitan Museum of Art and as far west as the former site of Seneca Village.

In their book, *The Park and the People* (1992), historians Roy Rosenzweig and Elizabeth Blackmar revealed new information about Seneca Village that brought this important, pre-Park community to life.[3] The community began in 1825 and became the earliest and longest stable community of African-American property owners in urban America. It was comprised of about 250 African-American property owners, as well as some Irish and German immigrants, three churches, burial grounds, and Colored School #6, and all was established within the confines of the future Park at approximately West 81st Street to West 88th Street (above). Sadly, the community dispersed in 1857 for construction of the new Park, and they did not resettle in a new location.

52

THE RESERVOIR

When the *New York Times* reported that "a belt of humanity, a mile and a half in extent, circled the great Reservoir in the Central Park yesterday afternoon . . ." they were not describing a busy Saturday morning on the running track but the day on August 19, 1862, that pure Croton water entered into the largest man-made lake in the world. Cannon boomed and the Central Park band played as water—a virtual Niagara in force—gushed into the large basin, though the *Times* commented that after an hour it still seemed like "a speck in the ocean" and predicted that it would take several months to completely fill.[4]

By the early 1850s, it was obvious to a fast-growing population that in cases of drought or serious fire, the existing system was inadequate for the growing population. After searching the entire city, it was decided to site the upper reservoir above the lower one (now the Great Lawn). The Croton Aqueduct Board suggested it be named Lake Manahatta, but it was not officially named until 1994, when the City Council named it the Jacqueline Kennedy Onassis Reservoir, in memory of the former First Lady, who was often seen jogging along its path.

When it was completed in 1862, the 106-acre (96 acres in water surface) body of water was considered the largest man-made lake in the world with a depth of thirty-eight feet and the capacity to hold more than one billion gallons of water.

In 1856 Egbert Viele, the engineer and first designer of Central Park, had the good sense to change the shape of the reservoir's proposed parallelogram to a more naturalistic shape in keeping with his vision of a romantic landscape. Despite the gentler shape, Olmsted and Vaux still hated the reservoir for essentially chopping the Park in two disconnected sections. Olmsted described the walk around the reservoir as "unobjectionable" though "disappointing." Despite the "large scale" of water that he and Vaux wanted for the Park's water bodies, they deemed the reservoir's shape as "perfectly comprehensible and uninteresting after one or two visits of examination." In his opinion it lacked the mystery and surprise of the coves and inlets that the designers created for the Lake, the Pond, and the Harlem Meer.[5]

By the 1880s the reservoir system was deemed obsolete and Water Tunnel #1 was considered a necessity. In 1917, at the height of World War I, Mayor John Purroy Mitchell celebrated a new system by turning the valve that featured a 115-foot jet fountain, which the press christened "The Old Faithful of Central Park."

BRIDGE NO. 24 (ABOVE),
BRIDGE NO. 27 (RIGHT),
AND BRIDGE NO. 28 (OVERLEAF)

Olmsted and Vaux's original bridle path encircles the reservoir and features some of Vaux and Mould's most elaborate and elegant cast-iron Victorian bridge designs. Most bridges and arches in Central Park were assigned both a name and a number; however, the three reservoir bridges were not named.

CHERRY TREE ALLEÉS

Nearly 2,500 Japanese cherry trees were given to Central Park and Riverside Park in 1912 as a gift from Japan to commemorate the Hudson-Fulton Centennial. The trees were lost in transit, and a new lot had to be gathered together from the nurseries in Japan. The later consignment comprised many rare varieties, and miraculously the journey of three months didn't damage them. One hundred and seventy-four Yoshino cherries (above) were planted on the east side of the reservoir (they bloom in April), and 187 Kwanzan cherry trees (left, blossom in May) were planted along the west side of the reservoir. These are two of the most outstanding groves of flowering trees in the park.

PART FIVE

96TH TO 110TH STREETS

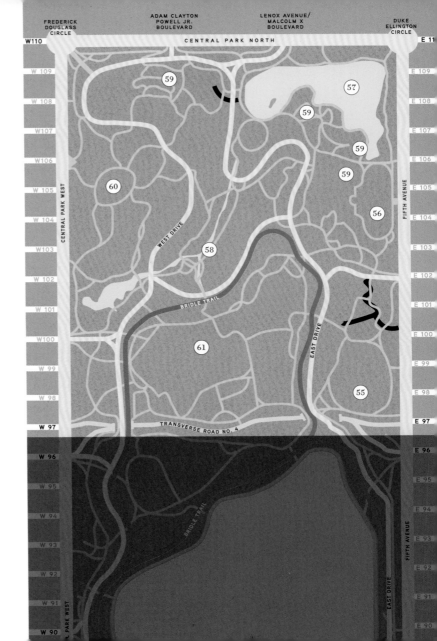

EAST MEADOW

When Olmsted and Vaux laid out the Park, they envisioned an arboretum as one of the most important features, even listing each genus and species in their written plan. Though the arboretum was never realized, the East Meadow possesses some of the finest specimen trees in the Park, particularly this magnificent American elm, believed to be one of the original Park plantings.

56

CONSERVATORY GARDEN

In 1898 an E-shaped conservatory and garden—hence the name Conservatory Garden—was created on the site of the former Park nursery where small plants and shrubs were cultivated for the Park horticulturists. In the 1930s Commissioner Robert Moses tore down the dilapidated greenhouses and hired designer M. Betty Sprout to design a new formal garden for the site. The six-acre Conservatory Garden features three different garden styles.

The Central Garden of the Conservatory Garden is entered through the cast-iron Vanderbilt Gate, once the entrance gate to the former Vanderbilt Mansion (now the Bergdorf Goodman store) on Grand Army Plaza. The central garden is in the Italian style with its rectangular central lawn surrounded by a series of geometrically shaped features: a semi-circular wisteria pergola, an elliptical jet fountain, and the spectacular double allée of white and pink crabapple trees. There are thirteen medallions inscribed into the pavement of the Wisteria Pergola, representing the original thirteen states. It is a subtle reference to the importance of this site in the American Revolutionary War.

The North Garden is in the style of an oval French parterre garden embroidered with scrolls of germander, which echo the larger planting beds that feature a spectacular display of tulips in the spring and Korean chrysanthemums in the fall. The *Three Dancing Maidens* fountain by Walter Schott was given to New York City in 1947 by the children of Samuel Untermyer, who had it at his Yonkers estate.

The South Garden, arranged in concentric planting beds, is in the style of an English perennial garden and features the most diverse seasonal plantings in the Conservatory Garden. In spring the garden comes alive with a dazzling array of bulbs and early perennials and flowering trees. In summer and fall, vines, annuals, and late blooming perennials—balanced for form, color, and texture—make this spot the most colorful in Central Park.

The South Garden is often referred to as the "secret garden" after the statues and lily pool, dedicated to Frances Hodgson Burnett, the author of the children's classic *The Secret Garden*.

HARLEM MEER AND THE CHARLES A. DANA DISCOVERY CENTER

The northern end of Central Park has a fascinating pre-Park history. Before Harlem became part of New York City in 1712, its boundary went as far south as 86th Street in today's Park. There were common grounds for cattle grazing, and a community of Dutch families that had intermarried and traded property as much as they had traded furs and tobacco. Several of these families also owned taverns that were adjacent to a major thoroughfare, known as the Kingsbridge Road, that ran through what is now the northern area of the Park where travelers could stop for a welcome rest for themselves and their horses. At the Charles A. Dana Discovery Center on the Harlem Meer that tradition continues by welcoming Park visitors with exhibits, tours, music and dance festivals, and the popular catch-and-release fishing program.

THE RAVINE

The walk from the Harlem Meer to the Pool was designed to be one of the great landscape sequences in Central Park. Today the Lasker swimming pool and rink obstruct the original experience, but after a flight of stairs behind the facility the path arrives at Huddlestone Arch, the most awe-inspiring feature in the Park. Made of massive boulders of Manhattan schist, the largest weighing almost a hundred tons, the arch is a marvel of Vaux's architectural skills, as absolutely no mortar was used to support the archway. Rather, it is held up by the pressure of the stones "huddling" against each other, hence the name Huddlestone Arch. Imagine the day in 1866 when the interior scaffold was removed, and the crew, holding their breath, witnessed the success of this brilliant engineering and construction feat.

Past the Huddlestone Arch, the sound of rushing water greets visitors at the Loch (Scottish for "lake"), the first of the Ravine's three magnificent cascades. This picturesque scene was created by the construction of a concrete wall, camouflaged by artfully placed boulders, over which New York City drinking water gracefully flows.

Charming woodland paths and rustic bridges lead the visitor through the natural swamp, an original topographic feature of the Loch, to another of the Ravine's **cascades** (opposite); the spray occurs as a result of the notches that were chiseled into the edges of the rock platforms.

Glen Span Arch (left) and its companion cascade signals the end of the Ravine, which opens up to reveal the Pool (overleaf), the Park's most intimate water body, so natural in appearance that it is hard to believe that it, too, is entirely man-made.

59

McGown's Pass, Fort Clinton, McGown's Tavern

THE BLOCKHOUSE
AND FORTS

An almost continuous band of rock outcrops crosses Central Park at 106th Street. The Kingsbridge Road was constructed through a narrow break in the rock, known as McGown's Pass, due to the nearby tavern, owned by the McGown family. The pass, the tavern, and the road played an important role early on in the American Revolution, when on September 15, 1776, the British attacked Manhattan Island. General George Washington, who had heard the cannon fire from his Harlem headquarters, rode immediately southward on the Kingsbridge Road and through the pass to rally his deserting troops on the shores of the East River. Washington and his men safely retreated westward to Harlem Heights, but the British marched up the eastern road to McGown's Pass. Within days, they claimed New York for the King and protected their stake in the city for the next seven years, stationing themselves at

the pass and surrounding areas in what is now the northern part of Central Park.

Forty years later roles were reversed during the War of 1812. After an attack by the British on Stonington Connecticut in August 1814, New Yorkers built military fortifications on the former British sites to defend against an attack from the north. Today the only remaining fortification is Blockhouse No. 1 (opposite) in Central Park.[1] When Olmsted and Vaux designed this area of the Park, the old fort was treated as a picturesque ruin with vines covering portions of the walls and landscaped with alpine plants and evergreens. Today the historic site of McGown's tavern is the composting operation where the products of the Park's horticultural maintenance are recycled and turned into compost that ensures a rich and healthy base for all new plantings.

60

GREAT HILL AND CHILDREN'S GLADE

The Great Hill was originally the site of British encampments during the Revolutionary War due to its strategic view of the North (now Hudson) River and its proximity to McGown's Pass. Olmsted and Vaux designed the promontory as a carriage turnaround. Today the Great Hill features a beautiful pastoral lawn and magnificent specimen trees. When the oval was restored in the 1980s, the designer created a mound, the peak of which would have been graced by a sunbeam at the moment of the vernal equinox had the surrounding buildings not existed. The woodland edge of the oval, the Children's Glade, is now the site of wonderful programs for families and a maze of country paths and quiet walks high above Central Park West.

61

NORTH
MEADOW

Central Park may be one of America's
most famous battlegrounds, as it has
had to struggle for its very existence
from the moment of its legal inception
in 1853. Just as construction work was
about to begin in 1856, the City Council
passed legislation to whittle away the
southern boundary of the Park from
59th Street to 72nd Street, and to bite
off an additional city-block-wide chunk
from its Fifth Avenue and the Central Park West borders. Only Fernando
Wood, one of the most corrupt mayors
in New York City history, intervened
and vetoed the measure that saved the
length and breadth of the landscape.

Today the Park is a National Historic
Landmark and a New York City Scenic
Landmark. Throughout Park history, the
North Meadow—the largest pastoral
scene in Central Park and the first land-
scape to be completed in the north

end—was under constant pressure to feature attractions and events that were not sympathetic to the designers' original intentions. A constant stream of suggestions for inappropriate projects both in the North Meadow and throughout the Park continued year after year. One of the bigger assaults came in 1918 during the dark days of World War I when a simulated battleground was proposed to raise money for "Liberty Loans," recommending the North Meadow be given over for "the most complete reproduction of . . . the actual trenches in France [then] occupied by American troops."[2] Some other proposals for the Park included: a World's Fair, a stadium for "noisy sports," a housing project, an opera house, polo grounds, a mausoleum for old movies, radio towers, airplane landings, a raceway, the straightening of all the drives, multiple requests for underground parking garages, and even one fleeting idea in the 1960s for a subterranean nuclear power plant. It is a miracle that Central Park exists as the pastoral retreat that it was originally designed to be.

EPILOGUE
"A MAGNIFICENT OPENING"

"To me it seems and always has seemed a magnificent opening. Possible together, impossible to either alone."

— Calvert Vaux, May 12, 1865

Calvert Vaux, the English-born architect and co-designer of Central Park, wrote this message in a letter to his once and future partner, Frederick Law Olmsted, describing how he had felt about their greatest collaboration—Central Park. At the time, Olmsted had left New York, first for the war, and then in order to pursue mining interests in California. Vaux was trying to convince him to join him in New York on the design of a project for the nearby City of Brooklyn. This design, which Olmsted agreed to join Vaux in creating, would eventually become Brooklyn's great Prospect Park.

"A magnificent opening" is an apt description of Central Park. By now, Sara Cedar Miller has taken you on a grand and expansive tour of the Park. You have seen images of Manhattan's great urban oasis from Columbus Circle all the way north to the Harlem Meer. Central Park is a marvel of landscape architecture, an open expanse of crafted natural splendor within the core of one of the most densely developed cities in the world. However, it is also a magnificent opening to the modern era of urban parks. Throughout New York, the United States, and the world, parks bear the imprint of Olmsted and Vaux's first creation.

Central Park could be thought of as the first major urban park with what could traditionally be described as "American" values. Although the concept of parkland in cities predated Central Park, the major European parks, such as Paris' Bois du Bologne and London's Hyde Park, were royal hunting grounds that had been opened to the local gentry. Other parks, including New York City's first park, Bowling Green, were either formed from unused land, or were market squares or agoras that had been deeded to the public. By contrast, Central Park came about precisely because urban living demanded forethought in creating natural space. Innovative thinkers, including William Cullen Bryant, the editor of the *Evening Post* and one of the earliest advocates of urban parks; Andrew Jackson Downing, landscape designer and mentor of Olmsted and Vaux; and Andrew Haswell Green, the first head of the Central Park Commission, all understood that parkland needed to be set aside for a rapidly growing young city.

The winning design for Central Park was selected through a public and democratic competition. Green, in particular, was the strongest advocate on the Commission for Olmsted and Vaux's winning design, which would become known as the Greensward Plan. Central Park, for all its natural beauty, is not a farm, estate, or royal land deeded to the City, but is instead foremost a triumph of landscape design. As you have seen in this guide, the Park is a sculptural and cleverly formulated masterpiece of architectural beauty. Decades of

Prospect Park

heavy construction went into its creation, but upon its completion, the sheer magnificence of the Park made clear the need for designed open space in other cities. Central Park became the model for urban park planning, and it continues to play this role today.

Naturally, Olmsted and Vaux were the first to spread the principles of Central Park beyond its borders. At Prospect Park, they honed their skills in a new terrain, one which was wider and covered in old-growth forest. Huge rolling greenswards like

the Long Meadow were interspersed with lakes, forests, and rolling hills. They would go on to collaborate on several more projects within New York, including Fort Greene Park in Brooklyn, and Morningside Park and Riverside Park in Manhattan. They would also design Ocean and Eastern Parkways, in Brooklyn, the earliest examples of pedestrian- and bicycle-friendly pathways that today we refer to as "greenways." In fact, Central Park's loop drive and well-disguised transverse roads presage the landscaped parkways and grade

Prospect Park

separation of traffic of twentieth century America.

After dissolving their partnership in 1872, Vaux would remain in New York, designing homes, apartments, landscapes, and institutions including the Metropolitan Museum of Art and the Museum of Natural History. Olmsted, the more public figure, would leave New York, taking commissions

and spreading the gospel of Central Park to cities across the growing nation. Boston's Emerald Necklace, the park system of the city of Buffalo, Chicago's 1893 World's Columbian Exposition, and the grounds of the United States Capitol building, were some of Olmsted's later park designs. These and the thousands of managed urban parks that have

since been created worldwide all bear some imprint of Central Park, the world's first truly urban park.

Today, Central Park again stands as a global leader in park management. This is less of a fait accompli than it may seem at first glance. In the 1970s, New York City had fallen into a deep fiscal crisis, and with it, there was no money left in the municipal budget for even basic maintenance of the park system. Even Central Park, the city's "flagship" open space, had fallen into grave disrepair. The Great Lawn and other meadows had become dust bowls; and its sculptures and majestic structures had been vandalized, covered in graffiti, and in some cases stolen from the Park. The fantastic structures of the nineteenth century, including the Belvedere Castle, were abandoned ruins. Olmsted and Vaux's signature pastoral pathways had become havens for muggers and drug dealers. When I first joined the Parks Department as a teenage summer worker in 1973, morale was at an all-time low. My first job was to pick up litter on the Lower East Side, and I observed firsthand the ways many employees stole time and shirked responsibility.

By the late 1970s, it had become clear that Central Park needed a new style of management and care to ensure a viable future. Things had gotten so desperate that some civic leaders suggested turning Central Park over to the federal government. Advocacy groups had formed to start raising funds for basic park services, and even more, to develop a base of concerned neighbors who would care about the Park. Meanwhile, Mayor Edward Koch and my predecessor, Gordon Davis, began to professionalize the department, now that New York had started to recover from the fiscal crisis. They had appointed borough Park commissioners for the first time, creating a layer of accountability. They also founded the Urban Park Rangers, a team of dedicated young "parkies" who would lead tours, enforce the Park rules, and help keep our parks clean. The Rangers were also a training ground for future Park managers—I was a member of the first class of one hundred Rangers, and many of my fellow alumni rose to senior staff levels in our park system today.

Fittingly, the person who told me about the Urban Park Rangers was Betsy Barlow Rogers, a seminal figure in Central Park's history. As a recent college graduate, I was interviewing her for a neighborhood newspaper, as she had just been appointed the first Central Park Administrator in more than seventy-five years—a position Olmsted himself thought necessary to the vitality of the Park. With her background in city planning, she began to seek partners in her effort, reaching beyond the then-limited public funding, towards the private sector. The idea of private citizens helping to care for a public facility was not new—the concept had been applied to museums, the performing arts, universities, and hospitals for generations. But as municipal budgets and management for parks declined, it was clear that we needed to develop similar innovative management and planning responses. Rogers helped found the Central Park Conservancy in partnership with Mayor Koch and Commissioner Davis, with the citizen leadership of Arthur Ross, Richard Gilder, and George Soros, among others, to help restore the Park to its historic preeminence as the world's greatest urban park.

The success of the public/private partnership with the Central Park Conservancy was obvious and immediate. The Sheep Meadow was restored in 1979–80, Bethesda Terrace and Belvedere Castle the following year, Heckscher Ballfields the year after that. The Conservancy brought programming to the Park, and converted the Dairy into a visitor center. A restoration and management plan was published. Perhaps most important, young graduates of college-level horticulture programs were recruited as "horticultural interns," laying the foundation for the crucial work of restoring the Park's green infrastructure. Volunteers began to get involved with the Park, and organizations such as the Conservancy Women's Committee were created to raise funds for the Park.

As the Conservancy took on more and more of the day-to-day oversight, it became clear that the partnership with the City needed to be codified.

With the leadership of Parks Commissioner Henry J. Stern and Central Park Conservancy Chairman Ira Millstein, in 1998 the City signed a historic management agreement with the Conservancy, later renewed in 2006. Under this contract, the Conservancy contributes more than eighty-five percent of the funding for the day-to-day care of the Park, and is also charged with the responsibility of offering educational and cultural programming about the Park. The City continues to provide for the Park in the form of security, road maintenance, and utility costs and pays the Conservancy a management fee, along with contributions toward capital improvement. One of the greatest benefits of this lasting partnership is that it transcends changes to mayoral administrations and park commissioners. The Conservancy model establishes a continuous group of advocates for their Park. Moreover, it is again a uniquely "American" model of management. European cities, with a higher municipal and federal tax

base, have until recently not had a need to seek out private contributions that can supplement for tax revenue. (That, however, is changing, as even European cities have seen a diminishing base of public support for parks.)

As was the case more than a hundred years earlier, the lessons of Central Park first spread across the East River to the nearby Prospect Park, which formed its Alliance in 1987. We had found a "magnificent opening" of private support for our parks. We tapped into a city filled with people who cared about their parks, and were willing to contribute their money and time to this cause. Today, with encouragement from Mayor Michael R. Bloomberg, more than eight hundred groups and 55,000 volunteers are actively beautifying parks in New York City. Altogether, they raise more than $90 million every year for park programs and improvements and donate 1.6 million hours in volunteer labor. In fact, the public/private partnerships that were pioneered in Central Park have become world-

Prospect Park

wide models. City officials from all over the world come to Central Park to see if they can replicate its success in their parks, meeting with Park Administrator and Conservancy President Douglas Blonsky and his talented and dedicated staff. (Doug, who began his Conservancy career as a landscape architect, is truly one of the great professional park managers of the world.)

Why is it, then, that Central Park has come to be the nexus for innovative park management for more than 150 years? New York has a unique relationship to its parks, dating back to the initial call for designs that led to the Greensward Plan. Most New Yorkers do not have backyards of their own. Parks are where New Yorkers can get exercise and battle the effects of a sedentary lifestyle. In addition, they also serve as a place to contemplate and enjoy nature in the midst of a larger city; to be alone or in a crowd of 60,000 music lovers. Most of all, they are a place to do, as the Italian phrase goes, "farniente"— do nothing but watch the passersby, smell the flowers or fallen leaves, feel the sun or the breeze. Nowhere in the City is this more apparent than in Central Park, where on any given day, tens of thousands of people, and hundreds of their pets, take to the loop to run, bike, and rollerblade; to the fields to play sports; or to the lawns to lie down and read, or even take a nap outside.

Moreover, in an environment where cities must compete for residents and for tourist dollars, parks are preferred amenities. Here in New York, parks are no longer the blights that they were in the 1970s. Instead, they are featured prominently in real estate advertisements and commercial listings, magnets for new development and new residents. And as you can see when you visit Central Park, real estate alongside the Park is some of the most desirable in the world.

Central Park is a haven for New Yorkers, and a beacon for millions of tourists who visit our city each year. That is why it will continue to be an international leader in urban park management, and billions of people throughout the world will continue to use parks that have been inspired by this "magnificent opening." I hope that you will enjoy your next visit to the Park.

Adrian Benepe
Commissioner, New York City
Department of Parks & Recreation

ENDNOTES

INTRODUCTION

1. See Sara Cedar Miller, *Central Park, An American Masterpiece*, New York, 2003, for a more comprehensive guide to the history and design of Central Park and a list of the primary and secondary sources for further study.

2. Frederick Law Olmsted, Letter to the Board of Commissioners of the Central Park, January 22, 1861, quoted in S.B. Sutton, ed, *Civilizing American Cities: Writings on City Landscape*, New York, 1997, 13-14.

3. Arthur C. Danto, quoted in *Encounters & Reflections: Art in the Historical Present*, New York, 1990, 141.

4. "Preliminary Report to the Commissioners for Laying out of a Park in Brooklyn, New York: Being a Consideration of Circumstances of Site and Other Conditions Affecting the Design of Public Pleasure Grounds," 1866, quoted in Sutton, 15.

5. Frederick Law Olmsted and Calvert Vaux, "A Review of Recent Changes, and Changes which have been Projected, in the Plans of the Central Park," Letter I, "A Consideration of Motives, Requirements and Restrictions Applicable to the General Scheme of the Park," January 1872, quoted in Frederick Law Olmsted, Sr., *Forty Years of Landscape Architecture: Central Park*, eds. Frederick Law Olmsted Jr. and Theodora Kimball, Cambridge, Mass., 1973, 248.

6. Letter I, *Forty Years*, 250.

7. From a document titled "Calvert Vaux Duly Sworn," 1864, quoted in Francis R. Kowsky, *City, Park & Country: The Architecture and Life of Calvert Vaux*, New York, 1998, 122.

8. "Preliminary Report to the Commissioners for Laying out of a Park in Brooklyn, New York: Being a Consideration of Circumstances of Site and Other Conditions Affecting the Design of Public Pleasure Grounds" 1866, quoted in Albert Fein, *Landscape & Cityscape: Frederick Law Olmsted's Plans for a Greater New York City*, New York, 1967, 106. For a discussion of Olmsted's theories on the psychological effects of landscape, see Charles E. Beveridge and Paul Rochereau, *Frederick Law Olmsted: Designing the American Landscape*, New York, 1995, 34-39.

9. Fred B. Perkins and W.H. Guild, *The Central Park: Photographed with Descriptions and A Historical Sketch*, New York, 1864, 16.

10. "Description of a Plan," quoted in *Forty Years*, 221.

11. Calvert Vaux to Clarence Cook, June 1865, quoted in Kowsky, 120.

12. Board of Commissioners of the Central Park, *Fifth Annual Report* (1861), 48.

13. "Description of a Plan," quoted in *Forty Years*, 232.

14. I owe a great debt of gratitude to Carol A. Hrvol Flores for her book, *Owen Jones: Design Ornament, Architecture, and Theory in an Age in Transition*, New York, 2006, and her patience and attention to my many questions regarding Vaux and Mould's designs in Central Park. Owen Jones, *The Grammar of Ornament*, London, 1856, quoted in Flores, *Owen Jones*, 98.

15. *Sixth Annual Report of the Board of Commissioners of the Central Park, January 1863*, "Report on Nomenclature of the Gates of the Park," 1862, 125–36.

16. For the best document of the Central Park Conservancy plan to restore and manage Central Park, see Elizabeth Barlow Rogers et. al., *Rebuilding Central Park: A Management and Restoration Plan*, Cambridge, Mass., and London, 1985.

PART ONE

1. *New York Times*, June 21, 1928.

PART TWO

1. *New York Times*, December 16, 1925.

2. *Sixth Annual Report of the Board of Commissioners of the Central Park*, January, 1863, 45.

3. Fred. B. Perkins and W.H. Guild, *The Central Park Photographed with Descriptions and A Historical Sketch*, New York, 1864, 27.

PART THREE

1. For a discussion of the relationship of God and nature in nineteenth century America, see Barbara Novack, *Nature and Culture: American Landscape and Painting 1825-75*, New York, 1980.

2. On April 28, 2008, the 72nd Street Cross Drive was renamed Olmsted & Vaux Way in honor of the 150th anniversary of winning the design competition for Central Park.

3. The printed announcement of the unveiling is in the Stebbins Scrapbook at the New York Public Library. See also Department of Public Parks, *Third Annual Report*, 1874.

4. Frederick Law Olmsted, "Designers' Report as to Proposed Modifications in the Plan," May 31, 1858, quoted in Frederick Law Olmsted, Sr., eds. Frederick Law Olmsted, Jr. and Theodora Kimball, *Forty Years of Landscape Architecture: Central Park*, Cambridge, Mass., and London, 1973, 238.

5. *Eighth Annual Report of the Board of Commissioners of the Central Park*, 1865, 30.

6. *New York Times*, May 17, 1979.

PART FOUR

1. Gerald Koppel, *Water for Gotham: A History*, Princeton, 2000, 3.

2. In an interview with the author, November, 1995.

3. Roy Rosenzweig and Elizabeth Blackmar, *The Park and the People*, Ithaca, 1992, 65-73.

4. *New York Times*, August 20, 1862.

5. *Forty Years*, 239.

PART FIVE

1. For the most comprehensive history of the landscape that existed before the Park, see Edward Hageman Hall, *McGown's Pass and Vicinity*, New York, 1905.

2. "Central Park Trenches, Advertising Exhibition for Liberty Loans," *American Scenic and Historic Preservation Society Annual Report*, New York, 1918, 79. Henry Hope Reed and Sophia Duckworth, *Central Park: A History and a Guide*, 37-56.

LIST OF FEATURES

FINDING YOUR WAY INSIDE CENTRAL PARK

Almost every lamppost in Central Park has an embossed label that displays a four-digit number. The first two numbers indicate the closest cross street in Manhattan, and the second two numbers are oriented to either the east or west side of the Park (odd numbers are closer to the west side and even numbers are closer to the east side). For example, lamppost number 7314 indicates that the closest cross street to you is 73rd Street, and the 14 indicates that you are standing near the east side of the Park. The labels on lampposts located from 100th to 110th Streets still have four digits, but they drop the first digit (number one). Thus, lamppost 0107 is nearest 101st Street (01) and the 07 indicates that you are closer to the west side.

For any other practical information about visiting the Park, current programs for children and adults, events, tours, concessions, bloom schedules, park rules and permitting, accessibility, Central Park gift items, and about volunteering and donating to the Central Park Conservancy, go to the official website at **www.centralparknyc.org**.

ACKNOWLEDGMENTS

Central Park has been blessed with the extraordinary leadership of Conservancy President and Central Park Administrator Doug Blonsky and New York's Parks Commissioner Adrian Benepe, and it has been my own good fortune to have them not only as supporters of my work but also as friends for a quarter of a century. It is an honor to have them both as contributors to this book.

I am grateful to Lane Addonizio, Central Park Conservancy planner; Frank Kowsky, the eminent Calvert Vaux scholar; Carol Flores, associate professor in the College of Architecture and Planning at Ball State University; and Charles McKinney, chief of design for the New York City Department of Parks & Recreation, for their editorial suggestions and corrections to the manuscript. I am also grateful to my good friend Barry Lewis, the architecture historian and host of the Walking Tour series, which airs on the PBS channel Thirteen, for our many discussions about Central Park design and its importance in modern architectural practice and theory.

My sincere thanks to Vice President Terri Coppersmith for her support of this project; to the talented graphic designers, Jonathan Taub and Melinda Bush, who helped prepare the photographs for publication; to Alice Baer, who has taught me so much about writing and editing; to Ian Lefkowitz, who worked on editing a portion of the manuscript; and to Mara Richard and Valerie Thaler for their invaluable research assistance.

I have had extraordinary assistance from Chief Financial Officer Stephen Spinelli, who guided the legal aspects of the project and has always been a great supporter of my work. I am also grateful for the generosity of Conservancy friends and colleagues at Weil, Gotschal, Manges, Inc.—Ira Millstein, Ken Heitner, and Bernadette McCann-Ezring—for their professional services and personal support.

It has been a joy to work with everyone at Abrams. I am grateful to Eric Himmel, editor-in-chief, who took a chance on my first book about Central Park eight years ago and who, along with publisher Steve Tager, suggested this, my second book. My editor Andrea Danese has been a joy to work with. I have learned a lot from her editorial skills and creative thinking, and her patience with my constant changes has been most appreciated. Her assistant, Caitlin Kenney, was a tremendous help to me, for which I was most grateful. And finally, I wish to express my sincere thanks to the designers—Stuart Rogers and Sam Eckersley (Rogers Eckerlsey Design)—who devised an extremely elegant layout in which to fit the many pieces that finally came together in this book.

To my Conservancy and Parks Department colleagues and to the Conservancy donors, whose hard work, dedication, passion, and generosity are responsible for the beauty of the Park and thus for what has been captured in this book.

And to my daughter, Alison, for more than words could ever say.

Pages 2–3: An aerial view of the Reservoir and the cherry tree alleé on its west side.
Pages 4–5: An aerial view of Central Park looking north toward its 110th Street boundary. On pages 178–179 is an aerial view of the Park looking south toward the Central Park South boundary with the Empire State Building in the distance.
Pages 6–7: Sheep Meadow
Page 11: Bow Bridge

All photographs by Sara Cedar Miller, property of the Central Park Conservancy, except for the following:

p. 13: (c) The New Yorker Collection 2002 Lee Lorenz from cartoonbank.com. All Rights Reserved.
p. 14: Courtesy of the National Park Service, Frederick Law Olmsted National Historic Site, Brookline, Massachusetts.
p. 22. Private Collection
p. 60: The Metropolitan Museum of Art, Herbert Mitchell Collection, 2007
(2007.457.1-.3866) Copy Photograph (c) The Metropolitan Museum of Art.
p. 62. Herbert Mitchell Postcard Collection

Editor: Andrea Danese
Designer: Stuart Rogers and Sam Eckersley of
Rogers Eckersley Design
Production Manager: Alison Gervais

Library of Congress Cataloging-in-Publication Data

Miller, Sara Cedar.
  Seeing Central Park : the official guide to the world's greatest
urban park / by Sara Cedar Miller.
    p. cm.
  ISBN 978-0-8109-9628-1
  1. Central Park (New York, N.Y.)—History. 2. Central Park
(New York, N.Y.)—Pictorial works. 3. New York (N.Y.)—
Description and travel. I. Title.

  F128.65.C3M56 2009
  712'.5097471--dc22
                        2008045695

Compilation of illustrations © 2009 by Central Park Conservancy
Text © 2009 by Sara Cedar Miller

Published in 2009 by Abrams, an imprint of ABRAMS.
All rights reserved. No portion of this book may be reproduced, stored in a retrieval system, or transmitted in any form or by any means, mechanical, electronic, photocopying, recording, or otherwise, without written permission from the publisher.

Printed and bound in China
10 9 8 7 6 5 4 3

Abrams books are available at special discounts when purchased in quantity for premiums and promotions as well as fundraising or educational use. Special editions can also be created to specification. For details, contact specialmarkets@abramsbooks.com or the address below.

THE ART OF BOOKS SINCE 1949

115 West 18th Street
New York, NY 10011
www.abramsbooks.com